Building Financial Management
Capacity for NGOs and
Community Organizations

Praise for this book

'A deficit in financial management capacity is common in NGOs, and there is not much well-developed literature on the subject. John Cammack is a well-recognized author in the area of finance management of non-profits. This book has a lot to offer and suggests ways of developing capacity. John has pulled it off once again. Congratulations!'

Sanjay Patra, Executive Director,
Financial Management Service Foundation, India

'John Cammack's excellent book will serve as an invaluable resource for teachers, graduate students and practitioners of sound financial management for civil society organizations. This compact manual provides NGOs and small community organizations with capacity building measures that will allow for sustained growth in challenging circumstances.'

Professor Susan H. Perry, The American University of Paris

'Cammack's professionalism and extensive experience blends perfectly with his innate ability to be a powerful communicator. His writing is very much a dynamic dialogue between the practitioner eager to implement and the mentor providing both tools and vision.

'This book is an excellent, innovative tool which I would certainly recommend not only to NGOs but also to UN specialized agencies, academia and the private sector. This book was an absolute pleasure to read; if other training tools had even half of Cammack's style, learning would turn into practice with much greater ease and impact.'

Isabella Rae, Senior Programmes Manager,
Gorta-Freedom from Hunger Council of Ireland

'John Cammack's clear style of presenting complex ideas and the use of jargon-free language differentiates his book from other technical financial management resources. The book succeeds in providing an excellent framework of progressive stages to attain the "nirvana" state of financial sustainability and impact.

'*Building Financial Management Capacity* explains the importance of "hard" aspects of financial accountability, such as developing robust financial systems and implementing transparent financial processes. But the essence of this book is John's ability to emphasize and highlight "soft" issues. The case studies and practical examples illustrate the influence of organizational culture and human resource capacities on ensuring high-quality financial management.'

Gopal Rao, Director, Skills for South Sudan

Building Financial Management Capacity for NGOs and Community Organizations

A practical guide

John Cammack

PRACTICAL ACTION
Publishing

Practical Action Publishing Ltd
The Schumacher Centre
Bourton on Dunsmore, Rugby,
Warwickshire CV23 9QZ, UK
www.practicalactionpublishing.org

ISBN 978-1-85339-824-7 Hardback
ISBN 978-1-85339-825-4 Paperback
ISBN 978-1-78044-824-4 Library Ebook
ISBN 978-1-78044-825-1 Ebook

Cammack, J. (2014) *Building Financial Management Capacity for
NGOs and Community Organizations: A Practical Guide*, Rugby, UK:
Practical Action Publishing <http://dx.doi.org/10.3362/9781780448244>.

Since 1974, Practical Action Publishing has published and disseminated
books and information in support of international development work
throughout the world. Practical Action Publishing is a trading name
of Practical Action Publishing Ltd (Company Reg. No. 1159018), the
wholly owned publishing company of Practical Action. Practical Action
Publishing trades only in support of its parent charity objectives and any
profits are covenanted back to Practical Action (Charity Reg. No. 247257,
Group VAT Registration No. 880 9924 76).

Cover illustration: © Martha Hardy@GCI
Typeset by SJI Services, New Delhi

Contents

http://dx.doi.org/10.3362/9781780448244.000

Boxes, figures and tables

Boxes

Figures

Tables

Acknowledgements

Many people have helped in the preparation for the new edition of this book. Thanks to the Practical Action Publishing team: Toby Milner, Clare Tawney and Kelly Somers; and to Martha Hardy for the cover illustration. Thanks too, to the Oxfam Publishing team who edited the original edition, upon which the current text is based, in particular Alison Beaumont, Julie Jones, Kevan Ray, and Jackie Smith.

Thanks also to those who have read through and provided comments on earlier drafts of the text of the two editions: Adeola Akintoye, Freda Cammack, Stephen Cammack, John Cropper, Jacques Lauruol, Julieanne Porter, and Gopal Rao.

I am grateful to many people and organizations for help with the research for both editions, including Adeola Akintoye, Paul Anticoni, Mark Awiah, Jo Baker, David Black, Phan Kunthak Botum, Westone Mutale Bowa, Bill Bruty, Nick Burn, Jo Burton, Ken Carleton, Chilmba Chiyeñu, Mohammed Coulibaly, Ndeye Marie Fall Diagne, Abdoul Ma Ali Diallo, Tacko Sy Diop, Sally East, Nicola Elliott, Richard England, Janey Forgan, Sharda Ganga, Clive Gillam, Bronwyn Harris, Begay Jabang, Neil Jennings, Martin Johnson, Sheeraz Ahmed Khan, Dennis Khangalani, Anneli Kimber, Jacques Lauruol, Maren Lieberum, Harvey Livingston, Amédée Marescot, Aminulhaq Mayel, Alvin Mchemba, Lingalireni Mihowa, Gary Mitchell, Tendayi Moabi, San Moller, Damien Mosley, Besinati Mpepo, Dennis Mulenga, Muthoni Murlu, Stephen Murray, Samuel Musa, Clever Musonda, Felix Muyaso, Ayanda Mvimbi, Evelyn Naraga, Grace Nkhuwa, Alick Nyirenda, Mark Nyungula, Stephen Okafor, Vich Onn, Ousmane Pam, Sanjay Patra, Emma Porteous, Bryan Rambharos, Gopal Rao, Dorte Rasmussen, Mom Riam, Indy Sangha, Ernest Sessanga, Anisha Shah, Md. Moazzam Ali Shaim, Janet Shapiro, Ken Shoults, Emily Joy Sikazwe, Shamila Singh, Kirsty Smith, Hang Sophearyn, Clare Syanjelele, Timea Szeteiova, Karen Tidsall, and Roque Yap.

Contributing organizations include Afrique-Enjeux, Agir Autrement pour le Développement en Afrique, Amicale Socio-Economique Sportive et Culturelle des Agriculteurs du Walo, Amnesty International, Asylum Welcome, British Overseas NGOs for Development, British Red Cross Society, CECI Senegal, Centre for the Study of Violence and Reconciliation, Christian Aid, Cini Asha, Civil Society for Poverty Reduction, Copperbelt Health Education Project, Dan Church Aid, Evangelical Lutheran Development Services, FAMSA Welkom, Financial Management Service Foundation, InterChange Trust, Methodist Relief and Development Fund, Oxfam America, Matindi Youth Organization, Micro-Bankers Trust, PINORD, SCIAF, SOS Sahel, Stichting Projekta Surinam, VSO, Women for Change, and the Oxfam offices in Afghanistan, Cambodia, Haiti, Malawi, Philippines, Senegal, South Africa, and Zambia.

I am grateful to all the organizations who allowed me to use the stories about their financial management capacity building. Those without an organizational name are from my own experience working with organizations internationally.

I also thank those who have participated in workshops that I have facilitated, and organizations that I have visited as an adviser and consultant. Much of what I have learned from their combined wisdom is distilled throughout this book.

Last but not least, I thank Freda Cammack for her constant help and support in the process of writing this book.

John Cammack
Oxford, 2014

About the author

John Cammack works as an adviser and consultant, trainer, coach, and writer in the non-government organization (NGO) sector. He was head of international finance at Oxfam GB and senior lecturer in accounting and financial management at Oxford Brookes University. He now works with a range of international development and relief agencies. His website is www.johncammack.net.

His consultancy work includes: financial management and programme management reviews and capacity building for European and Southern-based organizations, working with NGOs and community-based organizations, and advising organizations on becoming 'fit for funding'. His participatory training includes: building non-profit financial capacity, financial management for non-specialists, training trainers (and specialist courses for training financial trainers), and developing communication between finance and non-finance staff working internationally and cross-culturally.

He is the author of *Communicating Financial Management with Non-finance People* (Practical Action Publishing), *Basic Accounting for Community Organizations and Small Groups* (Practical Action Publishing), and *Financial Management for Development* (Intrac). He co-authored *Financial Management for Emergencies* (www.fme-online.org). John is a professionally qualified accountant, manager, and teacher and specializes in the international not-for-profit sector. He holds an MSc in International Development Management, and an MBA.

Glossary

Accounting statements Financial summaries produced at the end of an accounting period, for example receipts and payments account, income and expenditure account (income statement), balance sheet.

Bank reconciliation A statement confirming that accounting records agree with the bank statement or pass book. It shows differences, such as cheques written but not yet presented at the bank, items paid into the bank (perhaps on the last day of the month) but not yet included in the bank account, standing orders, and bank charges.

Budget and actual statement A comparison of budgeted income and expenditure with actual income and expenditure, showing differences.

Cash advance Money given to an individual, usually a member of staff, for a work activity (for example travel) when precise details of the cost are not yet known.

Cash-advances/loans register A record of money given to an individual. It shows if, and when, the amount was accounted for.

Cash/bank book A record of money coming in and going out, in date order. 'Cash book' means both cash and bank transactions.

Cash-flow forecast A statement which forecasts the money coming in and going out over a period of time in the future.

Champion Someone who promotes or 'champions' a particular issue in a group or organization; for example, a member of the leadership team.

Communities Groups of people who benefit from the activities and services provided by a non-profit organization.

Community-based organization (CBO) Small non-profit group with a social purpose, sometimes run entirely by volunteers, based in the community that it serves.

Core costs The non-programme costs of an organization. Sometimes called **administrative costs**, **indirect costs**, **overheads** or **support costs**.

Donor An institution providing funding and/or other support to a non-profit organization. The donor may also be a non-profit organization.

Financial audit An examination of financial records and statements.

Financial management The use of financial information, skills, and methods to make the best use of an organization's resources.

Financial management capacity An organization's financial management, awareness, competence, and relationships which are used to make its overall management and programme activities effective.

Fixed assets Items owned for more than one year. Examples: buildings, vehicles, and computers.

Fixed-asset register A list of fixed assets, updated regularly.

Financing The various sources from which an organization receives its income.

Financing plan A longer-term planning activity that involves stakeholders thinking through the best way to finance the organization's objectives over the next 3–5 years.

Funding Income from an institutional donor.

Funding mix The balance between an organization's sources of finance, which help to diversify its income and make it more sustainable.

Leader The person responsible for the organization's activities. He or she may be the chair of the management committee or, in larger organizations, a senior staff member, sometimes called the chief executive officer (CEO), or director.

Leadership team The management committee, leader, and senior staff of a group or organization.

Longer-term planning See *Strategic planning*

Management audit (or systems audit) An examination of an organization's management, and financial processes and systems.

Management committee The body responsible for the management of a group or organization that meets regularly to decide policies. The committee may also be called the **advisory body, the board, executive committee, governing body,** or **trustees.** In small non-profit organizations the whole group may constitute the committee; in larger organizations the committee is made up of representatives of the membership.

Managers People responsible for a particular activity, department, or project. They usually have responsibility for the budget and staff.

Non-government organizations (NGOs) Non-profit organizations with a social purpose, usually with paid staff and volunteers. They vary in size and may be locally or nationally based.

Organization People working together in the non-profit sector for social objectives. It can be any size, from a small community group to a large national or international agency.

Partners Two or more organizations working together for a common purpose. A donor is often one of the partners.

Payment voucher A document attached to an invoice or receipt, to record details of payments.

Programme staff Staff working with a community-based organization, non-government organization, or charity, on activities with social objectives. In larger organizations, these staff might be advising or working with communities and/or their 'partner' organizations.

Reserves Organizational savings held to cover future shortages in funding and emergencies.

Restricted funds Money received from a donor for a particular purpose.

Stakeholders Groups and individuals, internal or external, who have an interest in the organization's well-being. They include community groups, partners, staff, volunteers, donors, government, suppliers, and the wider public.

Strategic planning 'A systematic process through which an organization agrees on its priorities and builds commitment to them among its key stakeholders. These priorities are selected as the most effective way of fulfilling the organization's mission, taking account of its changing operating environment' (MRDF, 2011). Also called 'longer-term planning'.

SWOT analysis SWOT considers strengths, weaknesses, opportunities and threats. It is a practical way of assessing either a whole organization, or a part of the organization (for example its financial situation). The information is used to determine objectives to build on strengths and opportunities, and minimize weaknesses and threats.

Umbrella group An organization co-ordinating and representing non-profit organizations, often nationally.

Unrestricted funds Money that can be used for any expenditure within the organization or project.

Introduction

Building capacity through financial management is a key way of achieving a more effective organization. With strong financial management capacity, the group or organization becomes more able to control its own affairs. This then leads to an improved programme of activities. Without good financial management, the future is often uncertain: it may be impossible to predict when money will be short and, crucially, it may become impossible to fund programmes.

This book presents practical ways to build financial management capacity in an international development context (although much of it applies to any non-profit organization). It describes good practice in the specific tasks of financial management – for example, planning and budgeting and financial controls. It gives examples of how groups and organizations build their own capacity. It also considers what leadership teams can do to guide their organization's longer-term direction (an activity sometimes called 'governance') and it describes other financial management aspects that can be built into an organization's structure to make it more sustainable.

It is written for non-government organizations (NGOs), larger community-based organizations (CBOs), and charities. For organizations with established systems, it provides challenging questions, both for their own organization and for the way in which they work with others. The book is written for chairs and members of management committees, leaders, chief executive officers, directors, managers, programme staff, administrators, fundraisers, and finance staff. It is a tool for large NGOs and donors working with their partner NGOs and CBOs. The content can also be used in training courses, and university and college courses for international development workers.

Building stronger financial management capacity is not difficult. If you follow the suggestions in this book, you should quickly start to see the impact. Your organization will be in a better position to show accountability, transparency, and credibility – all of which are conditions that donors consider priorities when funding programmes.

This is a book about building an organization's financial management capacity, rather than how to do accounting. Books that cover the technical aspects are listed in 'Written resources'. Some additional resources relating to those used in the book are available at www.johncammack.net (click on 'Resources').

PART ONE

Linking capacity building and finance

CHAPTER 1

Capacity building and finance

This chapter considers the link between capacity building and finance and offers some principles to guide organizations in building their own capacity. We will consider whose capacity can be built, what this means for organizations of various sizes, and some of the challenges that confront them.

Keywords: capacity building; financial management; management committee; sustainability; exit strategy

Building financial management capacity is a way of providing and maintaining an infrastructure. It can be the 'scaffolding' upon which to build the rest of the organization. If it is strong, the organization can flourish; if not, the organization may struggle or even collapse.

At one level, some basic financial skills are essential in order to keep accounting records and provide financial information that is required by law. But if financial management skills are used throughout the organization, they can in addition lead to empowered staff, improved sustainability, and better programme quality and impact.

It is not difficult for a group or organization to strengthen its financial management capacity, and it is not necessary to have an accountant in order to achieve this. Non-finance people, such as leaders, managers, and programme staff, can do this. The main tools are introduced in this book. By using them, you will start to see the impact. And you will create a model for your own staff to pass on to communities and partner organizations.

http://dx.doi.org/10.3362/9781780448244.001

Story: The annual meeting

Everyone arrived expectantly for the annual meeting of *Salud*, an organization dedicated to caring for people living with HIV/AIDS. Clients, members, staff, volunteers, and donors all agreed that it had been an excellent year, and they looked forward to hearing about future plans.

The meeting progressed with the usual business of reports and appointing the new committee. The annual review was very positive. Several of *Salud's* clients told their own stories, which were moving and inspirational. Later on a client asked: 'Why are you so effective at what you do? Everyone knows *Salud* has excellent staff and volunteers, but is there some other magic ingredient?'

The chair looked around the room and said: 'Our founders had a vision of what we could do, and they and others have worked passionately to achieve it. A few years ago we were in serious trouble. We got to a point where no donors wanted to fund us; morale was low, and our work was starting to suffer. Donors told us that they liked our programme but said they wouldn't fund us, because we had poor financial systems. This gave us a shock, and we knew we had to improve. It hasn't been difficult for us to introduce better systems, once we grasped the basic ideas.

'So, the "magic" is the passion for our work and our strong financial management. Now we don't have problems finding donors, and our programme decisions benefit enormously from up-to-date financial information. This is what allows us to keep on supporting people living with HIV/AIDS so effectively.'

Source: organizations in Africa and Asia

An approach to capacity building

What is capacity building?

'A systematic strengthening of the capabilities of an organization to perform its mission more effectively.'

Source: Tools for Self-Reliance, 2005

The Environmental Support Center and Innovation Network (2002) identifies nine principles for building capacity. These principles could be expressed as follows.

1. *Every organization is capable of building its own capacity.* It is very important to recognize that an organization is in charge of its own capacity building, and that its needs are unique. This gives better results.

2. *Trust between the organization and the capacity builder is essential.* Trust is at the centre of this relationship. The more trust there is, the more effective are these nine principles. Trust makes it acceptable to communicate openly, to risk disapproval, and to learn.

3. *An organization must be ready for capacity building.* Organizations can benefit from capacity building at all stages of their life. To be ready for capacity building, an organization needs to be:
   - open to change and willing to question itself;
   - able to describe its mission clearly;
   - willing to believe that capacity building will further its mission;
   - prepared to commit time and resources.

4. *Ongoing questioning means better answers.* The most successful capacity builders keep on asking questions, welcome both positive and challenging feedback, and encourage change. These create a climate where true understanding is welcome, not avoided.

5. *Team and peer learning are effective capacity building tools.* Individuals and teams are essential for capacity building. Facilitators may bring good ideas, but they don't have all the answers, although they can add greater momentum to the process.

6. *Capacity building should allow for different learning styles.* People learn in many different ways: some by doing, some by listening, some by talking, some by experimenting. Some think more visually, some more verbally. Good capacity building recognizes and uses these differences.

7. *Every organization has its own history and culture.* Understand and use the mission, the organizational culture, and the

environment of an organization. The more an organization's context is understood, the more powerful the capacity building.

8. *All the people and parts of an organization are linked together.* Understanding or changing an organization is much more likely to succeed if it involves people at different levels: staff, users, committee members.

9. *Capacity building takes time.* Capacity building that takes time is more likely to be absorbed into the organization's ongoing work. But short-term inputs, for example strengthening a particular skill, are also valuable.

These principles can be applied to all types of capacity building, including financial management capacity building. If improvements are to be sustainable, it is particularly important to remember that financial management capacity must be developed across every part of an organization. If it is developed only with finance people, it will not be enough.

Whose financial management capacity is being built?

There are four key groups who will benefit from financial management capacity building:

• members of the management committee;
• the leader and managers;
• non-finance and programme people;
• finance people.

What is a management committee?

The group of people, usually volunteers, who lead a non-profit organization and are responsible for it. In large organizations, the committee's members may represent different parts of the organization, meeting regularly to take policy decisions. In small groups, the whole group meeting together may take on the management-committee role. Whatever the size, there is likely to be a leader or chair, someone who looks after financial matters, and at least one other member. The committee members need to be aware of, and responsible for, the organization's financial well-being, and they should be accountable to its stakeholders for it.

It is important to make sure that everyone is considered when assessing individuals' needs for financial management capacity building, both in organizations and in community groups. Questions to ask include the following:

- Are those without formal qualifications included, when they have other relevant experience?
- Are women and men considered equally?
- Is training offered only to people who can read and write, ignoring those who work verbally?
- Are some groups ignored, for example people who are very poor, or older people, or those who have a disability?

Organizations of various sizes

Different-sized organizations need financial skills appropriate for their size, history, culture, context, and geographical setting.

- **Voluntary groups** with no paid staff or donor funding may need only a simple budget, a few accounting records, and some basic financial controls, for example making sure that two people sign cheques. They will not need complex systems.
- **Small to medium-sized organizations** with paid staff, premises, and maybe one or two donors will need a more developed budget, good financial controls, and accurate accounting records which can provide information to

donors in the format that they need. They may employ an administrator for day-to-day transactions and a professional accountant for putting the end-of-year accounts together. Some form of annual audit helps to build their financial management capacity and gives donors confidence in them.

• **Medium to large organizations** with more paid staff, their own premises, and many donors need well-developed accounting and financial systems, possibly a computerized accounting package, experienced accounting staff, and professional annual audits.

• **Large organizations** need well-developed financial systems, professional accounting staff, an organizational budget to which donors contribute, and a full audit.

Not all groups or organizations grow in size; but if they do, their financial needs will change. Part of the task of financial management capacity building is to identify when the next stage of development has been reached. Each organization is different. If the number of activities increases, for example when a donor offers a large amount of funding, it is worth assessing whether the financial management capacity is adequate before accepting the money. Organizations need careful management to avoid growing too quickly for their available capacity.

Appendix A offers a guide to the minimum financial requirements needed at different points in an organization's development.

Challenges of financial management capacity building

Building financial management capacity can bring enormous benefits to an organization, but it is a challenging process. It takes time to develop a full understanding of how each organization works.

Resources are not always available, so concentrate on ways of building financial management capacity that do not require high additional costs (see Chapter 11 for some suggestions).

Make it a part of your ongoing work (there are suggestions for this throughout the book). Sometimes two organizations can help each other with no cost involved. If there are costs, for example the costs of providing staff training, plan these in advance and discuss funding with donors.

When building any sort of capacity, it is important to be sure that the changes are 'embedded' into the organization as a whole. For example, make sure that more than one person is involved, and encourage people to write down their new ways of working, as part of a simple procedure. If only one individual is developed, he or she may, having been trained, decide to leave, and the organization will be no further forward.

When a donor is funding capacity building, an organization may not know how long its commitment is likely to last, and whether the funding will continue. Make sure that your organization itself 'owns' the capacity being built, so that any change of donor has less impact. The organization should be continually preparing itself for the eventual departure of each donor.

Donor organizations also need to prepare a clear 'exit strategy' well in advance of the relationship finishing, to help the organization to continue without damaging results. Each organization is unique and their needs should be reviewed with them and other stakeholders. Such a strategy might include: how the organization will be funded in future, whether the activities will still be carried out or handed over to another organization, whether successor organizations need training, and which assets the organization needs to retain. Ideally the capacity building inputs needed (for example financial and fundraising) will have been included from the start of the donor's involvement. This aims to make the exit as smooth as possible, and the organization sustainable or 'fit' for future funding.

CHAPTER 2

Assessing financial management capacity

In this chapter we consider how to assess an organization's financial management capacity in the key tasks of planning and budgeting, accounts record keeping, financial reporting, and financial controls. We also look at external audits and other organizational aspects that influence financial management capacity.

Keywords: financial management capacity assessment; planning and budgeting; accounts record keeping; financial reporting; financial controls; external audit

Assessing and building financial management capacity is one of many roles that leaders, managers, programme staff, and volunteers perform. It is often part of the broader organizational capacity building. People often recognize that an organization has weak financial skills, but find it difficult to identify what and where the actual problem lies. To start to build, we need a structure to help us to decide where best to focus our efforts. A key question to consider is 'Where are the gaps between what is actually done and what should be done?' You can then identify how these gaps can be filled.

The four specific tasks of financial management

Programme, sound financial management and effective community development go hand-in-hand. (Camfed, 2004)

What is financial management?
The use of financial information, skills, and methods to make the best use of an organization's resources.

Financial management is making sure that an organization manages its resources well. The four specific tasks shown in Figure 1 are the starting point for assessing and building financial management capacity. If you want to assess an organization, there are a number of questions in each section which, together with your knowledge about the organization, help to build a good overview.

Figure 1 Specific tasks of strong financial management

Planning and budgeting

The management committee and managers decide their objectives for the year and forecast the cost of achieving them. This is the annual budget. As the year progresses, the management committee and managers compare actual performance with budget forecasts. They can then decide whether any action is needed – for example, to increase or decrease spending, or undertake more fundraising. This regular monitoring of the budget also helps to manage donor funding and reporting.

Questions for an organization

- Are organizational objectives the starting point for the planning and budgeting process?
- Do the leader and management committee regularly compare budgeted income and expenditure with the actual income and expenditure, and take action where necessary, for example when donor funding may be lost if under- or overspending occurs?
- Is there always enough money to pay for salaries, goods, and services?

Accounts record keeping

A group or organization must keep accurate accounting records and up-to-date records of transactions. These are the basis of the information needed to manage the organization, and they will be used for internal and external financial reports.

Questions for an organization

- Is the record of money coming in and going out (sometimes called 'the cash/bank book') up-to-date and accurate?
- Is there a separate register to record loans or other money advanced to staff?
- Are there documents (for example invoices and receipts) for every transaction?

Financial reporting

Financial reporting includes producing the annual accounting statements and reporting to communities, partners, donors, and the government.

Questions for an organization

- Is it possible to identify funds that have been given for a particular purpose?
- Are financial reports submitted on time to donors and government?
- Are annual accounting statements produced as soon as possible after the end of the financial year?

Financial controls

The management committee and managers are responsible for financial controls which protect property and equipment and minimize the possibility of error and theft – for example, a system for authorizing expenditure when a purchase is made. Finance staff can advise on which controls to introduce, but the leadership team must make sure that the controls are working effectively.

Questions for an organization

- Are at least two people involved in transactions, for example authorizing payments and signing the cheques?
- Are the organization's bank figures agreed with the bank statements at least monthly? (This is sometimes called a 'bank reconciliation'.)
- Does someone, other than the person responsible for the cash, count it regularly?

External audit

Audit is an annual independent review which tests (among other things) whether the four specific tasks of financial management are working effectively. It is an excellent way of building strong financial management capacity.

Questions for an organization

- Is there an audit/independent review each year?
- Does the auditor make written recommendations?

- Are the auditor's recommendations prioritized and implemented?

The answers to all the questions in these sections should be 'yes'. If the answers are 'no', you should think about what is needed to build financial management capacity in that area.

Organizational aspects of financial management

The four specific tasks of financial management and external audit are not enough on their own. There are wider organizational aspects which will help you to run your organization professionally and build strong financial management capacity. These organizational aspects, shown in Figure 2, are essential for improving the organization's management and programme effectiveness.

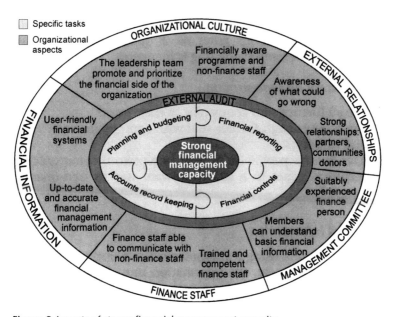

Figure 2 Aspects of strong financial management capacity

The management committee

One member of the committee should be responsible for making sure that financial issues are considered at each meeting. Other members should be competent to ask appropriate questions about any financial information presented to them.

Questions for an organization

- Is there one member who is responsible for financial issues?
- Can other members understand the financial information and ask appropriate questions about it?
- Does the management committee approve the annual budget?

Finance staff

In small organizations with no paid staff, the management committee's finance person does most of the financial work. Larger organizations recruit finance staff to do this. The level of staff will depend on the size and complexity of the organization. As organizations grow, more qualified staff may be required if, for example, funding is increased.

Questions for an organization

- Are all finance staff competent in their work?
- Are there enough finance staff with appropriate experience and training?
- Can finance people (or at least one person) communicate technical issues in a straightforward way to non-finance people?

Financial information

Whether you are using a computerized accounting system or a paper-based system, the information must be accurate and up to date. Information for a management committee does not need the same level of detail as information for a project manager who is dealing with day-to-day activities. Always present the information in a format that suits the needs of each different audience.

Questions for an organization

- Do the management committee, the leader, and managers receive up-to-date information?
- Does the information provided contain the appropriate level of detail for the different users?
- Do users find the information easy to understand?

Organizational culture

What is organizational culture?
The values, behaviour, and attitudes shared by people within an organization. They shape the way in which it relates internally and to its stakeholders. Culture can be described as 'the way we do things around here'.

The culture of the organization includes the priority given to financial issues. The leader, for example, must stress the importance of finance at meetings, and set a good example by making sure that his or her personal travel-expense claims are completed on time. Other staff will follow this lead. Programme staff and other non-finance staff should have a working knowledge of finance. Visiting donors are likely to be aware of a positive or negative 'culture', and may base their funding decision on it.

Questions for an organization

- Do the management committee and leader give positive messages about finance?
- Does the leader set an example in his/her personal accounting?
- Do programme staff and non-finance staff have a working knowledge of finance?

External relationships

Organizations should maintain good relationships and communicate openly with the people with whom they work, including communities, partners and donors. All stakeholders need to know about the financial aspects of your organization's activities. It is important to identify and plan for things that could go wrong: for example, the withdrawal of donor funding.

Questions for an organization

- Is your relationship with stakeholders open and transparent?
- Are your communities and/or partners given financial information in appropriate detail and format?
- Does the planning process consider what could go wrong?

The next stage

If you answer 'no' to any of the questions listed above, it is a sign that financial management capacity building may be necessary.

Having looked critically at your own group or organization, you may find that there are areas that need improvement. Prioritize this, but plan to do it over time, rather than all at once. Start with the areas that are most important and bring in outside help, if you need it.

We will consider each aspect of building financial management capacity in more detail in later chapters. They will show you the key approaches needed and will offer a 'toolkit' that you might use. The review of financial systems in Appendix B presents the main financial systems to show exactly where financial management capacity may need building. It is important to treat the basic questions in this chapter, and the more detailed review in Appendix B, as tools for building capacity, rather than a means of judging an organization. The aim of these tools is to help you to improve financial and programme capacity, and to be in a position where good management, growth, and effective fundraising are more easily achieved.

PART TWO

Building financial management capacity

CHAPTER 3
Planning and budgeting

The chapter looks at ways to build financial management capacity through planning and budgeting – the first of the four specific tasks of financial management. We will consider good practice in planning budgets, monitoring budgets, and forecasting cash flows. Finally we ask who might need to have their budgeting capacity built.

Keywords: budgeting; budget and actual statement; budget variance; management accounts; cash-flow forecasting; budget presentations

A budget is used to forecast income and expenditure. Budgeting is a valuable tool, because it helps organizations to manage their finances and develop their financial management capacity. Even small organizations prepare a budget when applying for funding, simply because donors usually ask for one. Many also monitor actual income and expenditure against what was planned, but some do not do this systematically. Monitoring is vital, both to keep control of the money, and to be sure that donor funding is being well managed.

Longer-term financial planning is considered in more detail in Chapter 9.

What is budget planning?

Budgets are planning tools. They help to express objectives in financial terms. They will cover the project period or a financial year. The budget is written down, sometimes with the help of a donor, and approved by the management committee. It is then presented to potential donors for funding.

---

http://dx.doi.org/10.3362/9781780448244.002

Organizations with one donor may have a simple budget prepared in their donor's format. Larger organizations with several donors may prepare their own budget and allocate donors' funds against different parts of their budget. Others may produce a series of donor budgets, although this makes monitoring for the whole organization more difficult.

Good practice: top 10 principles for budgeting

- Always start by deciding the objectives for the organization/activity together with other people. Ask the person responsible for each activity to prepare a budget.
- Use finance staff to provide technical advice, but not to decide priorities (unless it is their own budget).
- Be as realistic as possible. Add notes to the budget to show how calculations were made. Show whether income is 'guaranteed' or 'not yet confirmed'.
- Allow plenty of time before the start of the period/year and obtain approval for the budget from the management committee and/or donors.
- Show the agreed budget (and any alterations) to group members or staff. Tell them what they have to do to keep within the budget.
- If external funding is required, submit the budget (or part of it) to donors.
- Provide detailed budget-monitoring reports for those with day-to-day management responsibility, and a summarized report for the management committee.
- Monitor the budget against actual income and expenditure regularly. Take any necessary action. The management committee, leader, and managers should review these reports regularly. An example is shown in Table 1.
- Add notes to budget-monitoring reports, to explain major differences between the budget and actual income and expenditure.
- Keep donors informed of any changes to the budget (for example, if expenditure is more than the budget for one item and under budget in another).

Table 1 Example of a budget and actual statement

Southern Farmers' Support Organization
Budget and Actual Statement from 1 January to 31 October 20--

Budget items	Annual budget 1 Jan–31 Dec 20--	Budget 1 Jan–31 Oct 20--	Actual 1 Jan–31 Oct 20--	Difference 1 Jan–31 Oct 20--	% difference 1 Jan–31 Oct 20--	Notes
					%	
INCOME						
Dept of Agriculture	200,000	200,000	200,000	0	0	
NGO grant	600,000	500,000	450,000	(50,000)	(10)	1
Miscellaneous income	110,000	91,700	93,400	1,700	2	
Fees and charges	2,600,000	2,350,000	1,655,000	(695,000)	(30)	2
Total income	**3,510,000**	**3,141,700**	**2,398,400**	**(743,300)**	**(24)**	
EXPENDITURE						
Purchases of supplies	1,200,000	1,050,000	940,600	109,400	10	3
Salaries	793,000	665,400	654,800	10,600	2	4
Rent	1,200,000	1,000,000	1,000,000	0	0	
Vehicle/other expenses	105,000	87,500	98,200	(10,700)	(12)	5
Equipment	200,000	200,000	205,000	(5,000)	(3)	
Loan/overdraft charge	12,000	10,000	8,500	1,500	15	6
Total expenditure	**3,510,000**	**3,012,900**	**2,907,100**	**105,800**	**4**	
Total income less total expenditure	**0**	**128,800**	**(508,700)**	**(637,500)**		

( ) Shows more budget than actual for 'income' items, and more actual than budget for 'expenditure'.
No adjustment has been made for items received/paid for in advance or in arrears.
Notes: 1. Grant from NGO has not yet been paid. Should be received in November.
2. Market price of supplies temporarily fell, and so charges were reduced from August onwards.
3. Cost of purchases was less because of fall in market prices. Some supplies were bought in advance.
4. One member of staff left in September and will not be replaced until November.
5. Vehicle needed major repairs in March. Telephone charges increased and are not included in the budget.
6. Balance of loan interest will be paid in December.

What can a 'budget and actual statement' tell us?

The statement in Table 1 shows the different items in the budget listed under 'income' and 'expenditure' in the left-hand column. The next column shows the funds allocated to each item. The 'budget' items are then compared with 'actual' income and expenditure for January to October. The next column shows the difference between them. The % difference column shows any major differences, and the notes explain why items are under or over the budgeted amount.

In this example, the management committee or a manager might ask:

- Why has the NGO grant not been received (note 1), and what impact does this have on the financial situation?
- Are the NGO and Department of Agriculture grants restricted to particular budget items?
- What is the longer-term impact of the fall in market prices (note 3)?
- How much of the supplies have been bought in advance (note 3)?
- What expenditure could we reduce in order to stay within the actual income?
- Who will fund the telephone costs not included in the budget (note 5)?
- Who will pay the 5,000 for equipment bought but not budgeted for?
- How much money is in our bank account – can we keep going?

What is budget monitoring?

Actual income and expenditure is compared with the budget every month or quarter. A report – called 'budget and actual statement', or 'variance report', or 'management accounts' – is produced to show the comparison for each line of the budget. It shows the difference between budgeted income and expenditure and what is actually received and spent. You need to act if you see underspending or overspending, and if you have not received all the expected income.

Story: Budget difference

A Gender and Poverty project, funded by an Australian donor, has run for three years. The accountant and the co-ordinator worked together to make sure that the 'restricted' funding was fully utilized before the end of the funding period. They produced a monthly report to monitor spending against the approved budget.

One particular item was the stationery budget, which was set aside for workshop materials and looked as if it was going to be underspent. To avoid returning the money, the project decided (with the approval of the donor) to buy the stationery for the partners who were working on the project and to distribute it to them so that they could use these materials in future workshop activities. The restricted funding budget was all utilized without having to return the balance to the donor, thanks to the information highlighted in the budget report.

Source: Oxfam, South Africa

Cash-flow forecasting

In addition to the budget (which tells you if there is enough income to cover overall expenditure over the next year) and the monitoring report (which tells you how well or badly you are doing so far), a cash-flow forecast may also be useful. This tells you if you will have enough money to pay the bills as they fall due.

An administrator or finance person usually prepares the cash-flow forecast for the next six to 12 months. An example is shown in Table 2. A spreadsheet template, already programmed for preparing the cash-flow forecast and instructions on how to complete it, is available at www.johncammack.net (click on 'Resources').

Table 2 Example of a cash-flow forecast

Cash-flow Forecast for the Southern Farmers' Support Organization for the Six Months 1 January to 30 June 20--

PERIOD	Jan	Feb	Mar	Apr	May	Jun
	Currency	Currency	Currency	Currency	Currency	Currency
Money coming in						
Department of Agriculture	–	–	–	50,000	–	–
NGO grant	50,000	50,000	50,000	50,000	50,000	50,000
Miscellaneous income	9,000	5,000	9,000	9,000	10,000	10,000
Fees and charges	100,000	200,000	200,000	100,000	100,000	200,000
Total money coming in (B)	159,000	255,000	259,000	209,000	160,000	260,000
Money going out						
Purchases of supplies	80,000	80,000	120,000	120,000	100,000	150,000
Salaries	50,000	50,000	50,000	50,000	50,000	80,000
Rent	10,000	10,000	10,000	10,000	10,000	10,000
Vehicle/other expenses	12,000	12,000	12,000	3,000	2,000	5,000
Equipment	100,000	–	100,000	–	–	–
Loan/overdraft charge	–	–	–	–	–	3,500
Total money going out (C)	252,000	152,000	292,000	183,000	162,000	248,500
Opening balance **A**	22,000	(71,000)	32,000	(1,000)	25,000	23,000
Plus total money coming in **B**	159,000	255,000	259,000	209,000	160,000	260,000
Less total money going out **C**	252,000	152,000	292,000	183,000	162,000	248,500
EXPECTED CLOSING BALANCE (A+B−C)	(71,000)	32,000	(1,000)	25,000	23,000	34,500

Note: ( ) on 'opening balance' and 'expected closing balance' figures shows that there is a shortage of money in cash and at the bank.

What can a cash-flow forecast tell us?

The cash-flow forecast shows the money coming in and money going out over a future period. The 'expected closing balance' line tells us whether we have enough money for a particular month. A negative figure shows that we must arrange to pay 'money going out' items later, or receive 'money coming in' earlier. If this is not possible, a bank overdraft or temporary loan will be needed to keep the organization going. Without this review, we may not be aware that we will be unable to pay some of our expenditure (for example salaries) in some months. In the example shown in Table 2, the management committee or manager might ask:

- How up to date is the forecast?
- How will the negative balances be covered in January and March?
- Will the Department of Agriculture or the NGO donor give us their money earlier?
- Can we delay paying any of the money going out?
- What does the forecast for the rest of the year show?
- If we compare this forecast with the budget and actual statement in Table 1, we can see that all the expected fees and charges were not received, and some of the expenditure has been underspent or overspent. How will these factors affect the cash flow?

The three documents together – budget, budget and actual statement, and the cash-flow forecast – give the management committee, the leader, managers, and anyone else who needs it a clear picture of how financially sound the organization is.

Story: Cash flow

An agricultural organization had prepared a budget for the following year, assuming enough total income to cover all their expected expenditure. A major international donor had offered to contribute a large proportion of their funding, which they were keen to receive. But they knew that they would receive the income in two parts – the second part not until after the end of the budget year, even though they would have to pay for salaries, rent, and materials earlier. Staff thought that this would not be a problem.

One of their community groups suggested that they should examine their expected cash flow. This would help them to see when money would come in and go out, and when there might be shortages. They prepared a cash-flow forecast and found to their surprise that they had only enough money to cover expenditure for the next four months. After that, there would be three months when there would be no money at all, until the remaining funds arrived.

They approached the bank to ask for an overdraft. The bank refused, because they were a new organization. They then talked to their donor, to ask if they could have the funds earlier. After careful negotiation, the donor agreed to pay the second part slightly earlier. They also delayed paying two months' salaries, and did some local fundraising.

When planning for future years, the management committee requested a cash-flow forecast, together with each annual budget. They also decided to talk to their donors about their policies of not paying the second instalment of grants until the work was completed. One donor could not agree, and so the organization decided not to accept their funding again.

Source: From a training workshop, Serbia

Who needs to build budgeting capacity?

There are three main groups of people who need good budgeting skills: the management committee, leaders and managers, and finance people.

The management committee

Members are responsible for the organization's finances. They should approve the annual budget and annual financial statements, and regularly compare actual income and expenditure with budgeted figures.

Ideally, one member of the management committee should have some experience of financial work and take a lead on budgeting issues. Other members should have enough understanding of budget information to be able to ask questions.

If members do not understand financial information, it is important to arrange appropriate training in how to interpret it, and the kinds of question to raise. Training could take place during one of their meetings. It might be provided by a member, someone from another organization, or a donor. Sometimes donors are happy to provide and/or fund this type of training.

If none of the members has any knowledge of finance, it is worth thinking about changing the membership. The next time you appoint new members, make sure that finances are treated as a high priority and the necessary skills needed are brought into the management committee. The committee will need many other skills too: for example in fundraising, human resources, legal matters, programme activities, gender equality, and social diversity.

Information received. Sometimes members do not take finance seriously because they cannot understand the information they have been given. They might receive pages of figures which are difficult to absorb, especially if not seen before the meeting. Box 1 gives guidance for presenting budgeting

---

Box 1 How to present budgeting statements to committee meetings

- Identify why the information is needed: for example, to take decisions.
- Summarize the information; don't give all the details.
- Provide the budget and actual statement and details of your cash and bank position (or a cash-flow forecast) at least every three months.
- Make sure that the information is up to date and accurate.
- Use no more than one side of paper when presenting the information.
- Circulate information to members before the meeting.
- When talking at the meeting, select a few key points.
- Be clear and concise, using simple language, rather than accounting terms.
- Show the information visually, for example in a pie chart.
- Highlight any lighter parts – laughter helps people understand your points.
- Be brief – a few minutes is often enough.
- Make it easy for people to discuss and ask questions; encourage people to ask for more detailed information if they need it.

statements to meetings. The management committee should ask their finance people to follow these guidelines.

Leaders and managers

For organizations that employ paid staff, much of what has been said in the section above about management committees also applies to leaders and managers. They should prepare and monitor the budget for their work area and take any necessary action when they are presented with a budget and actual statement. An administrator or finance person will often prepare this information. The budget and actual statement may be the same outline information as presented to the management committee, but with more detail.

Leaders and managers do not always have the special skills needed to manage budgets. In such a case, they will need training to understand the format and content of a budget. Sometimes an 'umbrella group' or donor might provide this kind of training for community-based organizations and non-government organizations.

The leadership team should feel a sense of 'ownership' of the budget. The budget should not be seen as belonging exclusively to the finance people, just because they produced it. The more the leadership and managers are involved in, and trusted with, the design of reports, the more they will value them.

Finance people

Finance people often produce budget and actual statements in a format designed for their own purposes, rather than for the management committee, the leader, or managers. If, for example, a standard computerized accounting package is used, it may not produce the budget and actual statement in a way that is helpful for the organization. It is important that finance people understand the reasons why information is required. Box 2 shows how this information can be identified and produced.

Box 2 How to improve the presentation of budgeting information

Ask ...
- the management committee and managers what level of budget and actual statements they need – summarized or detailed – and involve them in the design;
- the management committee why they need the information, for example to help to take a specific decision;
- other organizations about the way in which they present information.

Then ...
- If the budget and actual statement is prepared manually, prepare the different versions as requested.
- If working with a computerized accounting package, explore the possibilities of producing the information in different versions.
- Try downloading (or if necessary re-inputting) the information into a computer spreadsheet program and adapting the information to the format that you want.
- In the longer term, if you are computerized, give non-finance people access to a 'read-only' version of financial data.

Finance staff do not need to be highly qualified in order to prepare budget and actual statements in different formats. Less experienced staff, however, may not know the possibilities available, so a member of the leadership team may need to take the initiative. Sometimes external auditors or donors will make suggestions.

As organizations grow, the information previously available is no longer sufficient to meet their needs. They can either try to manage with poor-quality reports, or they can invest in improvements. For organizations working with a paper-based system, this might involve training staff to present information in more easily understood formats. For organizations with computers, hardware and software may need upgrading and staff may need to be trained in the new systems. Changing software can be a big task, but may produce much better information with less staff effort. Donors can sometimes help to fund the changes (see 'Organizational aspects: financial information' in Chapter 8, page 90). If you are considering a change, you should seek advice from a qualified accountant or auditor.

Box 3 Planning and budgeting – common concerns

Concerns	Possible solutions
Our budgets are not prepared and approved before the start of the programme activity or financial year.	Encourage advance planning in order to set objectives for the next year. Tie the budget to the planning process and fix the meeting dates of the management committee. Make these dates known and ask for progress reports at each meeting. Arrange for the management committee meeting to approve the final budget several weeks before the start of the year.
All the budgetary decisions are taken by our finance officer.	Start the next budget cycle by arranging a meeting for those responsible for activities to talk about objectives and priorities. Convince them that these can only be achieved if the group take part in the budget process. If necessary, involve finance people or an external facilitator to offer training in preparing budgets. Have clear timetables, with budget formats prepared in advance.
Our budget does not fully represent our organization's values on matters such as gender and diversity.	Make sure that all appropriate voices are heard at the budget-planning stage. Finance staff may need training in 'gender budgeting' issues (see 'Web resources: Financial management' at the end of this book).
The objectives agreed in our original plan for this year are not fully reflected in the donor's budget.	If you discover this before the management committee approves the budget, and donor funding has been agreed, add the missing items, and make sure that all other objectives are included. If you discover it after budget approval, assess how vital they are this year, and talk to your donor if you need additional funding. If successful, ask the management committee to approve the additional items. If not, see if you can afford to pay for the additional items yourself.

Concerns	Possible solutions
Our budget and actual statements are always produced two/three months after the period has ended.	Talk to the finance people and ask why there is a delay and what can be done to avoid it. It may be that the statements are not prioritized (because people don't use them), or there may be resource-related problems: for example not enough staff, or outdated software.
No budget monitoring takes place.	Make sure that the management committee have budget monitoring on the agenda for each meeting. Produce a simple monitoring report monthly/quarterly for these meetings. Ask managers to use this too.
Our management committee show no interest in financial information.	Make sure that the information is designed for the right audience. Don't assume that one size fits all. A finance person on the management committee may raise the profile of finance.
Managers and the management committee members do not understand what is presented.	Organize training to help them to interpret the reports. If possible, ask finance people to do this, or invite an outside facilitator to attend one of the regular meetings.
Regular items such as electricity and telephone charges are only charged once or twice a year.	Include an estimate of these items each time a report is produced, so that it gives a truer picture. Ask finance people how they can help with this.
Staff who overspend their budgets are not asked to explain why.	Persuade the leadership team of the importance of this matter. Staff responsible for budgets should meet with their managers to explain any overspending.
Income promised has not been received. We may not be able to continue.	Act immediately. Warn the management committee. Contact donors. Prepare a cash-flow forecast to see how long you have money to carry on. Spend on essential items only.

CHAPTER 4

Accounts record keeping

This chapter looks at the records kept and some monthly routines completed in medium-sized organizations. It also suggests matters that a leader or manager might follow up when reviewing the monthly accounts.

Keywords: accounts record keeping; accounting records; cash/ bank book; ledger; monthly accounting routines

What would you expect to see?

The accounting system is likely to be based on one of the following:

- a paper-based system;
- a paper-based system supported by computer spreadsheets;
- an 'off-the-shelf' computerized accounting package;
- (for large organizations) a specially designed accounting package.

The following records are often kept, whatever system is in place:

- **Cash/bank book**, for each currency used. This gives a daily listing for money coming in and money going out, for cash and bank separately. Sometimes people call the main cash book 'petty cash'. However, petty cash may also refer to a small amount of money held by an individual in a separate office or location, to pay for small expenses and purchases.
- **Bank records** (bank statement or bank pass book).

- A record agreeing any differences between the bank statement/pass book and your bank book, called a **bank reconciliation**. It shows differences, such as cheques written but not yet presented at the bank, items paid into the bank (perhaps on the last day of the month) but not yet included in the bank account, standing orders, and bank charges.
- **Payroll details.**
- **Cash advances and loans registers.** These show details of sums advanced, repaid, accounted for, and still outstanding.
- **Records of funds given for a particular purpose**, what has been spent, and how much is left.
- **Invoices and receipts** that explain expenditure in the cash/bank book.
- Details of money owing to you (called **debtors** or **receivables**) and what you owe to others (called **creditors** or **payables**).

All computerized accounting systems must have paper-based information to back up the electronic information. Auditors always examine the paper records as well as computerized records. Larger organizations with more complex accounting requirements need additional records, for example:

- **A ledger.** This shows income and expenditure by type, for examples 'grants received' or 'travel expenses'. It gathers all the information about each type of income and expenditure in one place, unlike the cash/bank book which only shows the details in date order. This makes it much easier to find the total of what has been received/paid for each item and compare it with the budget. Computerized accounting packages are usually based on the ledger.
- **A journal.** This records adjustments in the accounts, for example because of errors. It is part of the ledger system of accounting. It allows users and auditors to trace adjustments made to the ledger.

These two documents need to be kept by a trained book-keeper. Organizations using them are also likely to have a computerized accounting package, and will produce an 'income and expenditure account' and a 'balance sheet' (see pages 44–45) at the end of the year.

Monthly routines

Introducing monthly routines helps to make sure that the accounting record keeping capacity covers everything that the organization needs. A finance person completes these routines, but the leader/manager then checks them, signs them off, and takes any further action that is necessary. The actual routines will depend on the size and complexity of the organization, and might include those shown in Box 4.

Box 4 Example of monthly accounting routines

Monthly routine	*Possible further action by leader/manager*
Update the cash/bank book.	Check that all transactions have supporting documents (for example, invoices or receipts). Count the cash and check that it agrees with the cash balance in the cash/bank book.
Agree the cash/bank book (your record) with each bank statement (the process known as a 'bank reconciliation').	Make sure you see the bank statement; check that the two records agree, and that the reasons for any differences are appropriate. Follow up any cause for concern.
Update details of cash advances and loans to staff. (Cash advances and loans registers may be used.)	Talk to anyone with a cash advance outstanding for more than a month.
List members of staff to be paid.	Approve payroll for payment. Make sure you know all the staff listed.
List organizations that owe you money and those that you owe money to.	Contact those who owe you money that have not paid for more than a month. Initial contact should be by mail/email; after two months, by telephone or personal visit.
Compare actual income and expenditure with the budget from start of the year to date.	Focus on large differences, find the reason for each difference, and take any necessary action.
List income/expenditure committed but not yet received/paid.	Check if the commitments change any of the 'actual' figures in the budget and actual statement. If any donor funds have not been received, contact the donor.
Calculate current cash-flow position.	Identify any shortages over the next few months and decide what to do.
Update stock records (if used).	Check stock records and make random checks at the warehouse on individual items. Check all the stock several times a year.
List any donor reporting needed over the next three months.	Make sure the information will be built into work plans and available on time.

Box 5 Accounts record keeping – common concerns

Concerns	Possible solutions
Invoices and receipts are not always available to back up our transactions.	Insist on receiving the correct paperwork before making any payment. Have separate files for 'money coming in' and 'money going out'.
Cash advances to our staff are not recorded and are out of control.	Start a cash-advances register to show amounts advanced, repaid, or accounted for, and what is outstanding. A senior person should review this each month and speak to those with unaccounted for advances.
Our accounts do not show whether 'restricted' funds have been used for the purpose given.	If you use a paper-based system, start a new book to record restricted funds, and make sure this is linked to expenditure. A computerized accounting system may have a facility for allocating the expenditure to a particular donor.
No one knows what money is due to be received.	A separate record of amounts due (sometimes called 'debtors' or 'receivables') will record any funding promised or invoices sent out. Keep a file divided into two halves; at the front, file details of money that should be received. When it is received, write the date, amount received, and reference; move this information to the back of the file. Review outstanding amounts each month and follow them up if necessary.
Staff do not know how our organization wants them to claim expenses, approve expenditure, and take advances.	If there is a written policy, see if it is understandable. If it is, circulate it. If not, consider writing down clearly how things should be done. In the longer term, putting things in writing is good practice for all financial tasks. Arrange some basic training on this procedure for existing staff, and make it part of the induction programme for new staff.

Concerns	Possible solutions
Only one person in our office can answer questions about invoices due to be paid.	More than one person needs to understand the records well enough to answer questions and take action, if the finance person is not in the office. Look at the jobs and find tasks that someone else can do regularly, so they too become familiar with the records in future. In a small organization the leader (or in a large organization the manager) should also be able to do this.
Our finance person is the only person who looks at the accounting records.	Introduce a system where the leader or manager sees the accounting records monthly. These should include at least the cash/bank book with invoices/receipts, the bank statement and reconciliation, and the advances/loans register. In larger organizations other records will be added. At the same time, count and agree any cash balance (this should also be counted and agreed weekly). The leader/manager should sign the records to confirm approval. If only one person sees the accounts, there is a danger of theft.

CHAPTER 5

Financial reporting

In this chapter we consider the different types of financial report needed for stakeholders. They include the annual accounting statements, which are often a legal requirement.

Keywords: non-profit financial reporting; annual accounting statements; receipts and payments account; income and expenditure statements; income statement; financial and management accounting; donor reporting; reporting to communities

The 'budget and actual' statement (shown in Chapter 3) is produced for the leadership team and managers. Organizations may also need the following financial reports for their external stakeholders:

- annual accounting statements;
- reports to donors (and 'narrative' reports on the programme activities);
- reports to government (for example, concerning tax or foreign contributions);
- reports to communities, and partner groups.

Each of these reports offers challenges to finance staff. Ideally the financial information is kept in a system that is flexible enough to present reports in different formats when needed, to suit internal and external users. Some computerized accounting packages can do this, but many organizations only use computer spreadsheets, or they have to produce these reports manually.

Annual accounting statements

Most organizations, even small ones, produce a statement at the end of their financial year, to report what they have done with the funds given to them. These are presented in two main ways:

Receipts and payments account

The receipts and payments account (sometimes called a 'cash account') shows a summary of all cash and bank money coming in (receipts) and going out (payments) over the last year. It is the simplest form of accounting statement. Items bought for longer-term use, for example vehicles or computers, are listed alongside the day-to-day items such as rent and salaries.

All the information for a receipts and payments account comes from the organization's own records. It shows:

- the amount held in cash and bank at the beginning of the year;
- plus money received (receipts);
- less money paid (payments);
- the amount held in cash and bank at the end of the year.

It does not show whether a surplus or a deficit has been made, only what money is left. The receipts and payments account is usually produced by small groups with a single purpose or activity and few staff. Its main advantage is that it can be prepared by someone who has not been trained in technical accounting.

Income and expenditure account

The income and expenditure account (sometimes called **account of operations**, **income statement**, **income and disbursement account**, **operating statement**, **statement of earnings**, or **statement of financial activities**) is an annual accounting statement to show what has happened over the last year. It shows the cash and bank amounts, but also additional items. For example, an amount due for payment in the year (for example the outstanding end-of-year telephone charge) will be included, even though it has not yet been paid. This means that the account shows a full 12 months' income and expenditure, and can be compared with the budget and previous year's accounting statements. Ideally the account should also show 'restricted' and 'unrestricted' funds separately (see Chapter 10, Box 18).

The income and expenditure account is usually presented with a **balance sheet**. A balance sheet shows what the organization owns (buildings, vehicles, equipment, and the amount in the bank account); what it owes (outstanding payments to suppliers and loans); and where the money has come from to fund what it owns (usually money built up from surpluses in previous years and any unspent donor funds held). These items are not included in the income and expenditure account.

The income and expenditure account and the balance sheet, and the records that support them, are more technical than the receipts and payments account. To prepare them you will need to employ a trained book-keeper, or ask an accountant or an accounting firm to help you.

A full explanation of these annual accounting statements is outside the scope of this book. Useful publications are listed in 'Written resources'.

Financial and management accounting

Some accounting is usually required by national law, which differs from country to country. The management committee and finance person must be aware of the appropriate requirements and they must keep records from the very beginning of the organization's activities. This information, called 'financial accounting', does not always provide all that is required for managing an organization and informing decisions.

Box 6 Differences between financial and management accounting

Financial accounting	*Management accounting*
Examples include annual accounting statements (for example, the income and expenditure account and balance sheet).	Examples include the budget, the 'budget and actual' statement and the cash-flow forecast.
Required by law.	Leaders and managers decide to produce it.
Shown to all stakeholders/donors.	Only used internally, but donors may see it.
Is usually audited.	Does not have to be audited.
Layout follows a standard format.	Layout designed to help users to take decisions.

Budgeting reports, for example, are produced for internal use, and usually there is no legal requirement, although donors often insist on a budget being produced. Budget information is part of 'management accounting'.

At some point in an organization's growth, more 'management accounting' information will be needed to help it to manage its activities more effectively. This may result in some extra financial work, although most computerized accounting packages can produce information in financial and management accounting formats. Sometimes a 'management accountant' is appointed specifically to develop these reports.

Financial reports to donors

Donors usually ask for reports on the use of the funds that they have given, often presented in their own format. These may include the following.

- A budget and actual statement, every quarter and at the end of their financial year, with notes to explain any changes (see Chapter 3).

- The audited annual accounting statements, for example the receipts and payments account or income and expenditure account and balance sheet.
- A separate report listing income and expenditure for parts of the programme that the donor has funded.
- Copies of (or original) invoices.

Reporting back to donors

It is essential to send reports to the donor by the agreed date. Include these reports in staff work plans, to make sure that deadlines are not missed. In addition:

- *Make sure there is consistency between the donor's budget format and the budget format that you use in your accounting system.* If your system cannot produce information in the donor's format, negotiate with the donor to accept your format, or think about ways of satisfying the donor but avoiding additional work. This makes reporting easier and maintains good relations with the donor.
- *Think about whether the level of your accounting skills is sufficient.* A large amount of new donor funding will increase your income and activities – and the systems required to support them. Make sure you have the appropriate capacity to manage and account for new programmes before accepting the funding. This includes the financial capacity at all the sites where you operate.

Financial reports to government

Some national (and sometimes local) governments will want full reports on the financial aspects of what you do, including:

- staff tax deducted from salary;
- organizational tax and sales tax;
- amounts paid to staff;
- contributions from international organizations.

Compliance with these regulations is vital, especially in countries where relations between non-profit organizations and government is sensitive.

Reports to communities

It is important to report to your communities and partner groups. 'Organizational aspects: external relationships' in Chapter 8 offers suggestions on how to do this.

Donors and government often ask for reports to be presented in their own formats. These may be different from your own. Try to minimize the work required for reports to your existing or potential stakeholders. Ask someone to give you advice on how to make your accounting system more efficient, so that it can provide reports in a range of formats.

Box 7 Financial reporting – common concerns

Concerns	Possible solutions
Our accounting statements are only produced ten months after the year-end.	Find out why they are late, and if there is anything you can do to produce them earlier. The delay may be due to your staff, or the auditors. Out-of-date statements are not so useful as current statements. Statements should be produced no later than six months after the year-end. There is usually a legal deadline by which the statements should be presented to the national authorities.
The management committee do not approve our end-of-year accounting statements.	Arrange the timing of their meeting to coincide with the production of the statements. Put the need for approval on the agenda, and circulate the accounts to members in advance.
Our computerized accounting package will not automatically produce the reports that we require for donors.	Talk to donors and ask if they are willing to accept what you already produce. If not, talk with someone who knows about the accounting system, and see if they can advise you. Think about buying or creating a system that will do what you want.
The government wants us to produce a statement in a different format from the one we use.	This may mean producing two statements each year. If you have a paper-based accounting system, this may involve considerably more work. If you have a computerized accounting system, investigate whether it can produce both formats from the accounting records. Could the information be downloaded to a computer spreadsheet which could then be amended?

Concerns	Possible solutions
We do not have a computerized accounting system, and preparing reports for different stakeholders takes too much time.	It may be possible to computerize your accounting to reduce the time taken, but don't rush it. Talk with your donors to see if they can fund the computer hardware and software, and training for staff.
Only the finance person prepares and reviews financial reports before they are sent to donors.	Financial reports need to be consistent with other reports about the programme. Someone other than the people preparing reports should review them, to make sure that they are consistent.
We do not understand national financial reporting guidelines and so we do not always follow them.	Get a copy of the guidelines (if available). Ask for advice from other organizations or a professional accountant in your country.

CHAPTER 6

Financial controls

This chapter considers financial controls and good practice in using them. It also looks at what happens if things go wrong, and how these risks can be minimized.

Keywords: financial controls; internal controls; trust and financial controls; fraud in non-profit organizations; top 10 principles for financial controls; minimizing fraud; whistle-blowing

Financial (or internal) controls are essential for any group or organization. They help an organization to prevent errors and the possibility of theft. Most importantly, financial controls help to protect reputations.

The leadership team and managers are responsible for making sure that there are good financial controls in place, and in some countries the management committee is legally responsible for this. If appointed, professional accounting staff (or external auditors) can advise on what systems are needed and how to introduce them.

What are financial controls?

The financial and management systems that aim to protect an organization's property and minimize the risk of error and theft.

Is trust enough?

In the non-profit sector, people sometimes say that controls are not necessary, as everyone trusts each other. Although trust is important, controls are needed in order to prove to stakeholders and others outside the organization that the leadership team are making effective use of money donated by individuals or organizations.

Story: Financial controls

Camfed Zimbabwe, established in 1993, is dedicated to fighting poverty and HIV/AIDS in rural communities by educating girls.

The communities where Camfed works had little experience of financial controls, so the organization offered training to help people to put controls in place. Camfed has a culture of trust and respect in these communities, and financial controls are a central part of this relationship.

The controls are there to protect everybody: the organization from theft or poor planning; volunteers and staff from false allegations or misunderstandings; and the communities themselves – as every dollar helps to improve the girls' education.

Introducing controls does not hinder Camfed's work in the communities, but rather helps it to build on the trust that has already been built up. Controls have helped Camfed to:

- understand its own organization better and take better decisions;
- strengthen its relationship with the Ministry of Education;
- attract more donations in cash and 'in kind';
- show people where the money is spent, and therefore increase their commitment to the task of educating girls.

Source: Camfed Zimbabwe

The key financial controls include the following:

- **Cash controls:** systems for managing cash amounts.
- **Bank controls:** systems for making sure that the bank account cannot be misused.
- **Budgeting and accounting controls:** systems that provide sufficient information to manage the activities of the organization.
- **Purchase and authorization controls:** making sure that different people are involved at each stage.

- **Management controls:** extra checks made by management.
- **Physical controls:** keeping property and equipment in good order and secure; and guidance on the personal use of items that the organization owns.

Developing good financial controls is central to building financial management capacity. To identify weaknesses in your organization, use the review of financial systems in Appendix B. Examples of good practice are listed below.

Good practice: top 10 principles for controlling cash

- Keep the minimum amount of cash needed for you to operate efficiently.
- Record all cash items received or paid in a cash book as soon as possible after the transaction has taken place.
- Issue pre-printed numbered receipts, with the organization's name, for any cash received, and keep a copy.
- Request a receipt and keep it when money is paid out in cash.
- Keep cash in a secure place – preferably in a lockable tin which is kept in a safe. If not, use a locked cupboard or drawer.
- A senior person should count the cash regularly and check that it agrees with the cash book. This person and the cashier should sign the cash book to confirm that the count has been made.
- Someone other than the cashier should authorize any large or unusual payments. Set a limit above which the cashier must obtain the approval of a manager.
- The person responsible for cash (the 'cashier') should not (ideally) be the one dealing with other accounting records.
- The cashier should check regularly how much cash is left and tell a senior person when more is needed for day-to-day operations.
- Make one person responsible for the control of cash at any one time. When a new person takes over, both people should agree and sign the cash balance.

Good practice: top 10 principles for controlling bank accounts

- Register bank accounts in the name of a group or organization – never in the name of an individual.
- Tell the bank that all requests for withdrawals (cheques, for example) should be signed by two people. Sometimes it is more practical to require 'any two signatories from three named individuals'.
- Never sign blank cheques, or expect others to do so.
- Each time that the bank statement is received (or the pass book is updated), check that the organization's own bank records in the cash/bank book agree with it.
- Write cheques for as many payments as possible, to avoid holding large amounts of cash.
- Transfer large amounts directly through the bank from one account to another.
- Pay money into the bank as often as practical, to avoid keeping large sums of cash on the premises. In rural locations, this cannot be done very often. Make use of people going to the town where the bank is, to pay money in. Cheques can sometimes be requested to avoid large amounts of cash building up. If cash is held, it must be kept securely.
- The person who is involved in the preparation of cheques should not also sign them.
- Keep cheque books in a safe, locked cupboard or drawer.
- Keep the fewest possible separate bank accounts, although some donors will insist that you keep a separate bank account for their funds.

Good practice: top 10 principles for budgeting and accounting controls

- Prepare the budget in line with organizational objectives before the start of the year, and ask the management committee to approve it.

- Produce the budget and actual reports as soon as possible after the end of the period.
- Add notes to explain large differences in the budget and budget and actual statements.
- Compare regular summaries of income and expenditure with the budget. Make sure that the management committee and managers monitor the summaries.
- Prepare a cash-flow forecast to show when shortages may occur.
- Record everything, keeping accurate and up-to-date accounting records.
- Make sure that there is a supporting document for every transaction (a supplier's invoice or receipt, for example), and file the documents in order.
- Keep a system to alert you when money is still owed to you.
- Record 'restricted' donor funding separately in the accounting system.
- Provide financial reports when required and include them in work plans.

Good practice: top 10 principles for purchase and authorization controls

- Make sure there is a budget for goods and services ordered.
- Allow only nominated people to place orders.
- Ask for at least three quotes for goods and services valued at more than a certain amount.
- Check goods and services received for quality before paying for them.
- Match invoices against original orders, and pay on original invoices only.
- Keep clear records of money owing and paid to other people.
- Do regular stock-takes of goods held, and check that they agree with stock records.
- Make sure a senior person authorizes expenditure before it is made.

- Have cheques authorized by a different person from the one who signs them.
- Ask self-employed individuals to provide evidence of their self-employed status before making a payment (so that if you don't deduct tax, you are not liable to pay it to the tax authorities).

Good practice: top 10 principles for management controls

- Allocate responsibilities to staff.
- Write job descriptions for staff and volunteers.
- Recruit suitably qualified staff and volunteers: check their references and qualifications.
- Identify and deal with staff who are not performing adequately.
- Make sure that everyone knows the policies and procedures. Write them down and talk about them regularly, for example in staff meetings.
- Develop staff and volunteers, for example through induction and training for new staff.
- Arrange an annual external audit.
- Act on the auditor's recommendations.
- Write minutes for all meetings with action points and names.
- Communicate openly with staff, volunteers, and other stakeholders.

Good practice: top 10 principles for physical controls

- Keep all premises locked and safe.
- Allow only authorized staff and volunteers to use premises and equipment.
- Keep an up-to-date record of items owned, and check it regularly.
- Register all items in the organization's name.
- Keep stock records for purchases, items issued, and the balance left.

- Count stock regularly and agree it with the records.
- Arrange insurance cover, if possible, for valuable items, including cash.
- Write clear policies on the use of equipment: for example, vehicles and photocopiers.
- Keep confidential information locked away.
- Use a safe for cash, cheque books, and other valuable documents.

When things go wrong

Non-profit organizations are often very trusting of their staff, but they need to recognize that theft, or 'fraud', can and does happen. Some of the most vulnerable organizations are those that prefer not to think about the possibility of fraud and therefore ignore it.

What is fraud?

Using deception to obtain an organization's money, goods or services for personal gain.

Examples of fraud include altering or forging cheques, making out cheques for personal payments, claiming for travel expenses not incurred, theft of cash, stock, or equipment and unauthorized use of vehicles, photocopiers or telephones. Often records are altered to try to cover up the fraud. Errors or mistakes are not fraud but, if not detected, can lead to fraud, for example by giving a staff member an opportunity to hide things and exploit the error.

The damage done by fraud can be calculated in terms of the amount stolen, but the biggest damage is to the organization's reputation. There is also a hidden cost of staff time and morale in creating new systems and repairing the reputation of the organization. Prepare your organization as if fraud is going to happen.

Knowing when things are going wrong

Although it is almost impossible to detect all frauds, tight financial controls will help to alert you when things are not right. There are a number of other accounting signs or clues to look out for:

- accounting records are inaccurate, corrected, and/or out of date;
- bank statements and 'bank reconciliations' are missing;
- invoices, receipts, bank statements, and other documents are often missing;
- financial and stock records contain many errors.

These are not necessarily fraud, but you should be suspicious.

Use regular budget monitoring reports to track whether the figures follow the expected pattern. Ask questions if, for example, the start of a project has been delayed, but its telephone and travel costs are still being paid.

Notice if people behave differently. If someone is suddenly buying lots of expensive items, think about where they might have obtained the money. Although there may be innocent explanations, if people are working long hours, not leaving their desks, not taking holidays, or are very tired and making mistakes, this could mean that they are covering up a fraud. Frauds are sometimes discovered when people are away sick. When you suspect something, this is an opportunity for you to investigate what is going on.

Story: Weak financial controls

The organization had grown from a small group of volunteers. It now had paid staff, its own premises, and a range of programme activities. It had always believed that it had good financial controls.

One day its bank telephoned to ask if the organization had written a cash cheque recently for 5,000 from its foreign-currency account. The signature on the cheque was OK, but the bank had noticed that it came from a separate sequence of numbered cheques.

The accountant knew immediately that she had not written it. The cheque was from a cheque book that had not been used and was kept in a locked cupboard. She only used foreign-currency cheques occasionally, so she would not have noticed this missing cheque for some time. Unfortunately the cheque had been accompanied by a letter of authority on headed notepaper, which the bank had taken as genuine and so had cashed the cheque a few days earlier.

On investigating the name of the person cashing the cheque, the accountant discovered that he had visited the organization some months before. She could only assume that he had been left in the office alone, the cupboard was left unlocked, and he had stolen the cheque and the headed notepaper. He then forged the cheque signatures from a cheque that had actually been issued to him. The man was eventually arrested and sent to prison, although the 5,000 was never found.

Source: a training workshop, Asia

Steps to minimize fraud

Introduce 'separation of duties'

Separation of duties affects every area of financial control. It aims to prevent errors and theft by making sure that one person is not responsible for the whole of any transaction, for example placing an order, authorizing a payment, and signing a cheque. There should be a different person to carry out each task.

Small organizations do not always have enough staff for work to be separated. They should involve someone else on an occasional basis, for example counting cash when an outside member of staff visits, or asking a local firm of accountants to make surprise checks. Being a small organization is not an excuse for poor financial controls. It is a reason to think carefully about ways to introduce them. You may need to ask a qualified accountant for more advice.

Make sure there are good financial controls

- The leader and senior staff should publicly make it very clear that theft of any sort is totally unacceptable.
- Explain to staff that controls are important for the protection of the organization and staff, even if sometimes hard to follow.
- Senior staff themselves should follow the rules strictly.
- The leadership team should implement controls and be prepared for possible fraud.
- Use induction of new staff to explain the fraud policy.
- Accurate and up-to-date financial information should be available in a user-friendly format.
- Leaders and managers should 'sign off' monthly accounts and make random checks on financial systems and agree the amount of cash with the records.
- Leaders and managers should follow up any complaints received.
- When recruiting staff and volunteers, always follow up references and check certificates of qualifications. Ask them about experience of fraud in previous organizations.
- Provide training in financial management.
- Arrange a regular external audit.

Make it easy for staff to tell someone if they are suspicious

- Create a culture that makes it easy for staff to share concerns – but this should be done responsibly and with specific evidence.
- Introduce a confidential 'whistle-blowing' scheme, explaining what this is and the sorts of issue that might need reporting.

What is 'whistle-blowing'?

Providing staff and volunteers with a procedure for confidentially reporting a concern about the conduct of a colleague, for example if mishandling of money is suspected. This would usually be reported to their manager, but a nominated senior member of staff or member of the management committee should be an alternative. The organization then has a duty to investigate the issue and take any necessary action.

Have a clearly defined policy to combat fraud

- Set up routine controls.
- Indicate how people can report their concerns.
- Specify when to tell the police.
- Identify the person who is responsible for any investigation.
- Define how an investigation can be conducted sensitively.
- Secure the documents that could be used as evidence.
- Describe how to record all incidents in a fraud register (see the next section).

This fraud policy should be made known to all staff. It should be updated after any theft or fraud is suspected or proved.

How to survive and respond

The organization needs to be able to learn from any incidents of theft or fraud. A key way to do this is through a 'fraud register'. This states the date and details of the incident, who was involved, the value of any lost property, a description of what happened, action taken, and lessons learned. You may need to check whether it is legal to keep anyone's name in such a register.

Make sure that any lessons learned are written down in full, and any necessary changes to the financial controls are made throughout the organization.

This may be a stressful time, and it is very important that those involved receive support from colleagues and friends. Members of staff who are not directly involved may feel that they too are suspected, so you need to rebuild their trust. This can sometimes be achieved positively by involving staff in a discussion about the possible risks and what could be done to avoid something similar occurring.

Organizations are sometimes reluctant to tell their donors about an incident of fraud; but generally it is better that donors hear about it from you, rather than someone else.

Box 8 Financial controls – common concerns

Concerns	*Possible solutions*
Our organization has grown recently, and our financial controls are inadequate.	Use the review of financial systems in Appendix B. If you have an external auditor, ask him or her to help you.
Only the cashier counts the office cash.	Ask someone other than the cashier to count the cash, on a different day each week. Calculate the current balance from the cash book and confirm that it agrees with the cash available. If not, find out why. Reassure the cashier that this is good practice and that you don't suspect them of anything.
I suspect that someone is using the vehicle for private journeys.	Use a vehicle log book to record all journeys, showing the destination, the mileage readings at the start and end of the journey, the day and time, and the reason for the journey. Check the log book against the vehicle reading.
Equipment in the office seems to be missing, but no one knows what should be there.	Write down a record of everything owned (an 'inventory') and keep it up to date. Check the items against it at least once a year.
Money that is owed to us is not received, and no one follows it up.	Issue invoices for goods or services promptly, and file a copy for reminders to be sent. Include a check on whether the debts are paid, and any follow-up, in the monthly accounting routines.
Our receipts are not pre-numbered.	Receipts could be issued for income and the money could be stolen, because there is no record of the missing receipt. Number all financial stationery so that it can be traced and keep a copy.

Concerns	Possible solutions
We are a small organization and know each other well. We don't bother about fraud.	Be aware of what could go wrong and build steps to minimize fraud. Organizations that ignore the possibility of fraud can be very vulnerable.
I am convinced that someone is stealing money, but there is no way of telling the organization.	Talk with your manager, a senior staff member, or a member of the management committee. Introduce a formal procedure for staff in these situations (a 'whistle-blowing' policy), and tell everyone about it.
One of our staff who stole money has now been dismissed, and we need to learn lessons from this.	Review all the financial systems. Write down what has happened in a 'fraud register'. Support staff and others who have been affected. Make sure that controls are in place so that it cannot happen again.

CHAPTER 7

External audit

This chapter discusses how an external audit can help to build financial management capacity. It considers the appropriate levels of audit for organizations of various sizes, the services you can expect from an auditor, and what documentation to expect or ask for.

Keywords: external audit; management audit; financial audit; audit opinion; independent review; management letter; audit report; audit and capacity building

External audit is a valuable tool of capacity builders. At best, annual audits offer an opportunity for an independent review of an organization's records and systems, with recommendations for improvements. Encouraging external audits and making sure that their recommendations are taken seriously will improve financial management capacity.

However, not all organizations will either have, or legally need, an audit. There are three categories of organization:

- **small,** where either an external audit is not legally required or it has not been thought necessary;
- **small to medium-sized,** where a formal legal audit may not be required, but a less demanding 'independent review' is done instead. Donors may however still require a formal audit;
- **medium to large,** where an audit may be required by law and/or by donors.

It is important to check the legal requirements in the country in which you work. Even if it is not legally required, your organization is likely to benefit from an audit to give it credibility.

Services you can expect from an auditor

An external auditor, from a firm of accountants, may offer different types of audit, some of which are described below.

Financial audits

A financial audit is an independent analysis of the accounting records and end-of-year accounting statements. At the end of this process, the auditor will give an 'opinion'.

What is an audit 'opinion'?

The auditor expresses an opinion at the end of the audit about whether the accounts give a 'true and fair view' of the organization's activity.

A positive (or 'unqualified') opinion is given in most audits. A negative (or 'qualified') opinion is less common, and a cause of concern for the organization. It suggests that something is not right. The organization's donors and other stakeholders will all see the opinion.

Management (or systems) audits

A management audit looks at the management and financial processes and systems. It examines how effective these are and makes recommendations for any necessary improvements.

Many audit firms will undertake both financial and management audits. The management audit, if well done, is more useful to help to build an organization's financial and management capacity. You should agree in advance on the type of audit to be provided, and include it in the terms of reference or 'letter of engagement'. A management audit may include the following components:

- an assessment of financial and management systems; for example, examining whether the authorization system is adequate, rather than merely identifying whether a particular purchase had the proper authorization;

- judging whether budgeting reports are in an understandable format;
- asking whether donor funding is meeting its objectives.

Not all external auditors would feel happy to assess particular aspects of a management audit; they may not even see it as their job. They will only do a financial audit.

If your auditor either does not do management audits or is unable to help you to build financial management capacity, you could use the information and questions in this book as a starting point. Ideally, it should be a joint effort between management and auditor, but management is ultimately responsible for building capacity. You might want to think about using an external facilitator to review your systems, if your auditor is not able to help.

Other types of audit, for example examining the impact of an organization's programme activities, are sometimes carried out only by larger audit firms.

Independent review

A review is less thorough than a full audit. It is done by someone who knows something about accounting but is not necessarily a qualified accountant. A key quality is that the reviewer is independent of the organization. He or she may undertake the review as a volunteer.

The process involves examining the accounting records and statements, but it is unlikely to cover a full management audit. It is suitable for small organizations only, and in some countries it may not fulfil legal requirements. Indeed some donors will require a full audit by a professional firm, which also gives the organization credibility.

The independent review will not always provide an 'opinion' or written recommendations, although it is still useful to ask the reviewer for their written comments. The review confirms the truthfulness of the accounts, but is less helpful for building financial management capacity.

This review is known by different names. It is sometimes called 'an independent examination', 'an inspection', or simply 'an audit' because it is difficult to tell the difference.

External and internal audits

An *external* audit is carried out by a qualified accountant or auditor. This is often someone from an 'accounting firm' or 'accounting partnership', whose key quality is independence from the organization that is being audited. When an employee of the organization conducts a review of financial controls, systems, and processes, it is an *internal* audit. Internal audit is not often used in the non-profit sector, except in large organizations. However, donors will sometimes want their own auditors to examine an organization's systems and records. This may be instead of, or in addition to, the annual external audit.

Using an audit to build capacity

Although independent examiners may not give written documents at the end of their inspection, if an external auditor is from an accounting firm, you can expect recommendations (sometimes called 'a management letter') and an audit report.

Recommendations

Towards the end of the audit, the auditor will raise concerns which have not been resolved, and will make recommendations for change. These will be shared in a draft letter written to the management committee or leader. The organization clarifies and, if possible, answers the points made. Some items are then deleted from later versions of the letter. The final version of the letter may include comments by the management on the points raised. It will include recommendations and identify matters that need attention either immediately or, more usually, before the next annual audit. An example is shown in Box 9.

Box 9 Extract from a management letter

1. A number of advances to staff were outstanding and not fully accounted for at 31 December. A more comprehensive system of financial control is required to make sure that these are followed up.

Management comment on paragraph 1
These advances have subsequently been accounted for in full. A new advances register has been introduced, to make sure that no new advances will be issued until accounts are provided for any outstanding ones.

2. Payment vouchers and connected documents have not been stamped to state that they have been paid. All of these should be stamped and dated, to avoid the possible reuse of a document.

Management comment on paragraph 2
The office has not held a 'paid' stamp. However, one has now been purchased and a system introduced to make sure that all documents are stamped.

3. Grant income received from international donors has not always been spent in the way the donor specified. The Centre's accounting records do not show income which has been given for a particular purpose identified separately.

Management comment on paragraph 3
We accept the auditors' observation that the accounting records do not separately identify all income received for a particular purpose. A new accounting procedure has been introduced which will rectify this.

We do not, however, accept that grant income received was not used for the purpose given. We understood that this income was unrestricted and as such it was used towards the general running costs of the Centre.

Source: Cammack, 2000

The management letter is a valuable contribution to the organization's ongoing development and capacity building. The management committee should receive it officially at their meeting (which the auditor may attend) and make sure that all the points are followed up. If there are a lot of recommendations, it is useful to categorize them as 'urgent', or 'important', or 'less important' and then start by implementing the urgent ones.

An audit report

This is a formal document which expresses the 'auditor's opinion' (see Box 10). It may draw attention to limitations in the scope of the audit (see paragraph 2 of Box 10). A negative or 'qualified' audit report may highlight a disagreement in the accounting treatment of a particular item which the organization has not fully explained (see paragraph 3 in Box 11). The 'except for' sentence (paragraph 4 of Box 11) suggests that apart from this one item, the accounting statements are not misleading. This opinion would be more strongly stated if the financial statements as a whole were misleading.

The audit report is attached to the annual accounting statements and circulated to donors and other stakeholders. It can also be used as a fundraising tool and given to potential donors.

Box 10 Example of an audit report with no negative comments ('unqualified' audit report)

We have audited the accounting records of the Lomtaka Health Care Centre, together with the financial statements for the year ended 31 December. These have been prepared in accordance with the accounting policies shown in the notes to the accounts. The audit was conducted in accordance with generally accepted auditing standards.

As with many similar organizations of this size, the procedures of internal control rely on the close involvement of the Centre's management. We have accepted the assurance of the Centre's management that there has been appropriate authorization and incurring of expenditure for the benefit of the Centre. Funds raised as a result of voluntary donations cannot be verified until they appear in the Centre's accounting records.

The financial statements have been prepared in accordance with National Accounting Standards. In our opinion the accounts present a true and fair view of the state of the Lomtaka Health Care Centre's affairs for the year ended 31 December.

....   Date: ....

Auditors

Source: Cammack, 2000

Box 11 Example of an audit report with a negative comment ('qualified' audit report)

We have audited the accounting records of the Lomtaka Health Care Centre, together with the financial statements for the year ended 31 December. These have been prepared in accordance with the accounting policies shown in the notes to the accounts. The audit was conducted in accordance with generally accepted auditing standards.

As with many similar organizations of this size, the procedures of internal control rely on the close involvement of the Centre's management. We have accepted the assurance of the Centre's management that there has been appropriate authorization and incurring of expenditure for the benefit of the Centre. Funds raised as a result of voluntary donations cannot be verified until they appear in the Centre's accounting records.

While conducting the audit, we have found examples of grant income received which has not, in our opinion, been used for the purpose for which it was given. These items were not accounted for in a way that we would normally expect of an organization of this type.

The financial statements have been prepared in accordance with National Accounting Standards. Except for the comment in the previous paragraph, in our opinion the accounts present a true and fair view of the state of the Lomtaka Health Care Centre's affairs for the year ended 31 December.

....   Date: ....

Auditors

Source: Cammack, 2000

How to find an auditor

Sometimes it is not easy to find a suitable auditor, especially one who has experience of dealing with non-profit organizations. You could ask for a recommendation from other organizations, or from donors, who sometimes keep a list of accounting firms and partnerships, or go directly to a local accounting firm – but ask for references from their clients in non-profit organizations, and follow them up.

Box 12 External audit – common concerns

Concerns	*Possible ways forward*
No audit takes place in our organization.	Check whether an audit is legally required. If so, find an auditor, not forgetting to include the fee in the budget. (Donors will often pay for this.) If not, ask your organization if an external audit would be beneficial for building capacity. If so, arrange it.
We need an auditor, but we don't know where to find a good one.	Ask similar organizations, or your donors. Standards vary, so it is important to meet the auditor who will do the audit (not just the firm's partner), to discuss the kind of approach they will take. Ask, for example, 'Do you provide a management audit?', 'What would a management audit involve?', 'How long will the audit take?', and 'May I speak to some of your clients?'
Our management committee do not appoint the external auditor.	Include 'appointment of auditor' on the management committee's agenda each year, well in advance of the end of the year.
The same auditor has been with our organization for 20 years. Everybody knows her and likes her.	It is difficult to be objective after so long, especially if the auditor is liked. If there are other auditors available locally, think about changing. If not possible, see if another auditor from the same firm could do the audit.
Auditors only look at our financial records, never at the systems or impact of the work.	Decide what you want from an audit. For all but small organizations, it is important to audit financial and management systems, as well as financial records. This will provide recommendations for building financial management capacity. Some auditors are also willing to assess the impact of your work, but you will need to ask them to do this.

Concerns	Possible ways forward
The auditor's junior staff always conduct our audit; the senior staff don't get involved until the very end.	This tends to be usual, as it reduces the costs. If you think this is affecting the quality, talk with the auditors' senior staff or think about changing the auditors.
Our auditor provides an 'audit report', but never gives us any recommendations.	Ask the auditor to provide written recommendations at the end of every audit. Include this in the terms of reference for the audit, given to the auditor.
Our auditor provides only verbal recommendations.	Ask the auditor to put the recommendations in writing.
Our auditor's recommendations are never taken seriously.	If the recommendations are seen only by the management committee, examine the minutes and find out what happens to the recommendations after the meeting. Paid staff or volunteers should be responsible for following up each point. The management committee should insist on receiving progress reports at each meeting, until all the recommendations are implemented.
We have an annual external audit, but both our donors want to send their own auditors.	Ask the donors if your external audit report would be enough for their purposes. If not, welcome the donors' auditors as well.

CHAPTER 8

Organizational aspects of financial management

In this chapter we identify five organizational aspects that can either help or hinder financial management capacity building. These are the management committee, finance staff, financial information, organizational culture, and external relationships.

Keywords: management committee; finance staff; communicating financial information to communities and partners; communicating financial information to stakeholders; capacity building of finance and non-finance staff; organizational culture; risk management

The following organizational aspects are shown in Figure 2 in Chapter 2.

Organizational aspects: the management committee

Some members of the management committee may be unaware of their responsibility for the quality of the financial side of their organization. In some countries it is a legal requirement. The tasks that they need to consider in order to fulfil this responsibility include the following:

- setting objectives;
- approving and regularly monitoring the budget;
- approving the annual accounting statements;
- appointing the auditors;
- receiving and acting on the audit report and recommendations;

- making sure there is adequate money and longer-term finance;
- appointing adequate finance staff;
- making sure there is a high standard of financial management;
- reporting to donors on what has been received;
- complying with national legislation and regulations.

Members of the management committee in smaller organizations may be involved in the day-to-day financial tasks, but in many organizations they are not. It is essential therefore that one member is specifically responsible for looking after the financial side of their work and bringing regular reports and decisions to the whole management committee.

You need as a minimum someone who is honest and numerate, who shares the organization's values (for example, its commitment to diversity and gender equality), and who will work with others to achieve the aims of the organization. Finding a suitable finance person can sometimes be difficult. Ideally, he or she should be someone with experience of dealing with financial matters. For larger organizations this could be a qualified accountant. Where it is not possible to find anyone suitable, some organizations advertise within their own and other known organizations and networks; consult their donors; find a staff member from another organization; or train an existing member. Alternatively, a committee member takes on the role but works with a paid person who provides advice. Or someone is paid (if allowed by national law) to act as an adviser to the management committee instead of being a member of it.

Someone may be appointed who has the practical skills but no previous experience of working with a non-profit organization. It is important then to make sure that training is available to help the person to understand and fit into the organizational culture as quickly as possible.

This financial responsibility of the management committee must be fulfilled. Organizations which do not have someone giving this advice to the senior decision-making body are less likely to be sustainable.

Understanding the information

The management committee have a controlling and question-ing role, so members must have a basic understanding of what they are seeing in financial reports. At least one or two members should ask questions (for example: 'Why have we not spent the budgeted amount on materials?' or 'Will our donor still pay for this item, even though it's overspent?') If they do not ask questions, finance staff or an external facilitator may need to make the information clearer and train members in interpreting it.

The management committee have a key role in controlling the organization. The financial information can highlight major problems, for example:

- There is not enough money to pay the bills.
- We need more funding.
- Our programme is not operating as expected.
- Money may have been stolen.

If the management committee is not using the financial information, the leader or manager must ask themselves why not. In the immediate future the leader or manager must make sure he or she understands it. A scheme to encourage management committee members to regularly meet with staff might help to build this capacity. (See Story: 'Buddy' system for staff and management committee members.)

Story: 'Buddy' system for staff and management committee members

We are a non-profit organization. Our non-executive management committee (trustees) take the major decisions. The members are volunteers and meet only four times a year, and have been recruited with a variety of backgrounds and skills. We recognized that the trustee group as a whole was not close to the everyday activities of our organization. This made it difficult for them when discussing business and taking decisions at meetings.

We have recently introduced a 'buddy' scheme, where trustees meet with senior staff members. Staff and trustees were matched by drawing the names from a hat. Each pair was originally asked to meet three times a quarter between the meetings. This was difficult to fit in and has now been reduced to twice a quarter. We meet at a place convenient for us both, and have found it is useful to meet outside the office, sometimes in a local café. The meetings last about an hour to an hour and a half.

The meeting between a trustee and finance officer means both can discuss the issues they struggle with. After one meeting the trustee said they were shocked at how little they knew about the finance role and the areas of responsibility for the officer. The one-to-one nature of these meetings means that trustees are able to find out the areas of concern for the management and understand first hand the operational difficulties faced in running various parts of the organization. This has proved difficult in the past because all meetings have been in formal groups with a set agenda.

Although we are still at the early stages, we hope that trust and relationships between staff and trustees will be improved. After the initial round of meetings, trustees and staff will be changed around so over time each trustee will have spent time with each senior staff member. We hope to build financial capacity by asking trustees about the financial information they receive and how it might be changed to improve their understanding, and to discuss whether trustees with their new financial understanding of the organization might act as fundraisers and ambassadors.

So far the scheme has produced many benefits: it is easy to discuss issues informally, and find what each of us struggles with; and key issues can be identified more easily in one-to-one meetings.

Source: InterChange Trust, United Kingdom

Finance sub-committees

Larger organizations usually have a separate 'finance sub-committee' which takes responsibility for many of the financial tasks. This sub-committee would include members of the management committee and staff. It will have more time to look at the details. But even where a sub-committee exists, the management committee still needs a full report at each meeting and makes decisions such as approving the budget, appointing the auditors, and receiving the audit report.

Organizational aspects: finance staff

It is important that finance volunteers and paid staff are fully trained and able to do their job competently. Different-sized organizations need different skills, as follows.

Voluntary organizations: a group of volunteers, with at least one of their members responsible for finance, with or without training or experience.

Small to medium-sized organizations: one paid member of staff with a job description that defines finance as either part or all of their job. This person may not be a financial expert, but some of the work needs professional accounting skills. One option is to use an accountant for work such as the end-of-year accounting statements: someone who is either employed on a part-time basis or hired from a firm of local accountants.

Medium-sized to large organizations: a trained book-keeper (someone keeping the accounting records) or an accountant is appointed, capable of more technical accounting. In these organizations, someone other than the book-keeper may be responsible for other financial tasks, for example handing out cash (which is the job of a 'cashier').

Large organizations: with more complex accounting systems, there is usually at least one accountant (sometimes called a 'financial controller') who has qualified for the role by taking professional accounting exams. He or she is usually a member of a recognized accounting institute, either in the home country or abroad.

The level of staffing depends on the complexity of your activities. Organizations working with several donors and community groups are likely to need more financial staff. Lists of typical financial tasks and necessary qualifications and experience are shown in Tables 3 and 4.

Table 3 Typical financial tasks

Tasks	Cashier	Book-keeper	Accountant / Financial Controller
Cash and bank handling			
Be responsible for office cash and keeping it safe	✓		
Issue petty cash to team members, based on authorized documents	✓		
Keep a record of all petty cash issued, with supporting vouchers	✓		
Issue advances to team members, based on documents which have been authorized by the correct person	✓		
Keep a record of advances and account for them	✓		
File vouchers for all money coming in and money going out	✓		
Pay wages to national staff	✓		
Notify book-keeper/programme manager when a further amount of cash is needed	✓		
Prepare cheques from invoices and payment requests	✓		
Book-keeping			
Keep a cash book and update it regularly		✓	
Make sure adequate documentation is available to support all income and expenditure		✓	
Make sure income and expenditure are coded accurately		✓	
Prepare wages for national staff		✓	
Agree the bank statements with the cash book, at least monthly		✓	

Tasks	Cashier	Book-keeper	Accountant / Financial Controller
Prepare monthly summary of accounts		✓	
Provide monthly cash-flow reports		✓	
Receive and summarize expenditure of team members		✓	
Make sure transfers between accounts are correct		✓	
Get explanations for items not accounted for satisfactorily		✓	
Help the programme manager in budgeting		✓	
Provide regular 'budget and actual' information for budget managers so that they can monitor expenditure		✓	
Provide reports on income and expenditure as required		✓	
Train team members in accounting for expenditure		✓	
Keep a record of all fixed assets		✓	
Accounting/financial control			
Review and introduce new accounting and financial control systems			✓
Manage accounting staff			✓
Count the cash held by the cashier regularly and agree with the accounting records			✓
Manage the funds in the bank account(s) including transfers			✓
Maintain a strong business relationship with bankers			✓
Monitor the cash advances system			✓
Visit programmes to provide advice on accounting and financial control systems			✓

Tasks	Cashier	Book-keeper	Accountant / Financial Controller
Look at the accounting implications for any new programme proposal, before it is submitted for funding.			✓
Make sure that programme managers prepare programme and administrative budgets. Provide technical support where needed.			✓
Meet with programme managers to make sure budgets are adequately monitored.			✓
Arrange production of other management information, as required.			✓
Communicate with donors to make sure that their reporting requirements can be fulfilled.			✓
Provide accurate reports to donors in their required format when they want them.			✓
Audit operational projects and arrange for external audit as required.			✓
Make sure audit recommendations are discussed and implemented.			✓
Provide training in accounting for programme staff and other team members.			✓
Interpret financial information for non-accountants.			✓

Notes:
1. In smaller programmes, where only one 'financial' member of staff is employed, some tasks will need to be given to other staff, e.g. the cashiering role.
2. The person who prepares cheques should not be a cheque signatory. If several finance staff members are employed, the most senior may sign cheques along with the programme manager, providing they are not involved in the day-to-day cheque preparation. If there is only one finance person, cheque signing should be the responsibility of the programme manager with another signatory.

Source: Cammack et al., 2005 © www.fme-online.org

Table 4 Qualifications and experience of finance staff

	Cashier	Book-keeper	Accountant / Financial Controller
Experience of the tasks in the job description – see Typical financial tasks (Table 3)	Essential	Essential	Essential
Numerate, methodical and accurate	Essential	Essential	Essential
Honest and trustworthy	Essential	Essential	Essential
Familiar with both an accounting package and Excel, indicating an ability to learn the organization's accounting software, if different		Essential	Essential
Experience of recruiting staff and providing one-to-one training			Essential
Supervisory and management experience			Essential
Experience of setting up financial systems			Essential
Able to communicate effectively both verbally and in writing			Essential
Formal accounting qualification			Highly desirable

Source: Cammack et al., 2005 © www.fme-online.org

Financial structures

In addition to recruiting and developing financial staff, organizations need to have clear management structures. If there is only one finance person, it is important to set clear boundaries and have a clear reporting line, especially if this member of staff is relatively junior. For example, this person needs to know if he or she is expected to represent financial matters at planning discussions and to be involved in the management's longer-term planning for the organization.

In larger organizations there may be a hierarchical structure. The senior member of the finance team would normally have formal training or an accounting qualification. He or she would usually take part in longer-term planning and decision-making

---

Story: Using financial skills

Asylum Welcome was founded about 10 years ago by a group of volunteers to provide support through advice and practical help for the increased numbers of refugees and asylum seekers in the UK. In the early days the voluntary treasurer was responsible for all the financial work. Office accommodation was provided free of charge in a community hall, and volunteers provided the advice work. There were minimal transactions. Individuals and local groups contributed funds.

After about four years, the work had grown. A number of organizations provided funds, staff had been appointed, and the organization rented its own premises. The services expanded to work with families and young people.

The accounting needs also increased. The voluntary treasurer still did some of the day-to-day financial work, and a qualified accountant was employed for half a day a week to complete the office accounting and budget reports. This made good use of the accountant's skills and was not too expensive. The accountant also prepared the year-end accounting statements. This was cheaper than using a firm of accountants. Volunteers helped with some of the routine financial tasks.

As the organization grew further, in addition to the part-time accountant, a financial assistant was employed for half a day each week to reconcile petty cash, record donations, and write cheques. This freed up the voluntary treasurer to concentrate on the financial policy issues.

Source: Asylum Welcome, United Kingdom

---

for the organization. It is important to have clear job descriptions for financial staff, and for the senior staff member to build the capacity of the finance team. The structure should always show a clear separation of duties.

Professional training for finance staff

Non-profit organizations often cannot afford to employ highly trained or qualified staff. One alternative is to train staff who deal with financial matters and so build individual and organizational capacity. Some training is 'on the job', but training courses are often available and may be more appropriate. They are sometimes provided by donors or 'umbrella organizations', and sometimes offered commercially. Ideally the training will be specific to the needs of the non-profit sector.

Some medium-sized and large organizations provide funding and/or time for their staff to study for professional accounting qualifications. The organization then benefits from their increased skills and motivation, often at a lower cost than recruiting a qualified accountant. Training agreements often require the person concerned to work for the organization for a certain number of years after qualifying. In reality, this can be difficult to enforce. Another way is to make sure that you do not invest everything in only one person, but look for ways to spread the benefits of that individual's training throughout the whole organization (see 'Maximizing workshop learning' in Chapter 12).

Communication about financial matters

Clear communication about financial issues strengthens the financial management capacity of a group or organization. It affects every part of an organization, for example:

- The members of the management committee need information and need to have their questions answered in a non-technical way.
- The leader and managers need appropriate information and explanations to understand financial statements and what they mean for the organization.
- Programme and finance staff need to make sure that the information is detailed enough for programme management and for donors.
- Communities, partners, and donors need clear, concise financial information and advice that they can understand.

In practice, weaknesses may occur, for the following reasons:

- Programme staff think that finance staff do not understand their work, and vice versa.
- Financial jargon and technical language are used and not understood.
- Finance is thought to be a matter for specialists.

- Information is prepared for accountants, but used by managers.
- Good communication skills are ignored when recruiting finance staff.
- Financial management skills are ignored when recruiting programme staff.

Achieving better financial communication. Finance people are not primarily recruited for their communication skills, but they need to communicate clearly, concisely, and in an encouraging way. This applies to all groups and organizations at whatever level: to the finance person on the management committee, to paid staff, and indeed to anyone who is talking about finance. Without these skills, an organization's financial management capacity is reduced, because people think that finance is only for specialists and no one else need bother. Good communication will enhance financial management skills, resulting in a more effective programme which attracts more donors. Always encourage good practice, as shown in Box 13.

Box 13 Good practice in financial communications

Do
- be clear and concise;
- focus on the key points;
- use simple language;
- explain any technical words;
- try to see the issue from the other person's point of view;
- keep people interested: ask your listeners 'is this making sense?'
- highlight any lighter parts – laughter helps communication;
- give plenty of opportunity to ask questions;
- encourage people to ask for more information;
- work with users to improve the clarity of financial information and systems;
- provide training where needed.

Don't
- use technical terms before explaining what they mean;
- talk for too long – a few minutes is often enough;
- confuse people with financial concepts and jargon.

Source: Cammack, 2012

An excellent way of improving communication is to arrange regular budget-monitoring meetings between finance and non-finance staff. Whenever a budget and actual statement or donor report is produced, arrange to have a short meeting soon afterwards to clarify the reports and discuss any concerns.

Story: Short, regular meetings

Programme and finance staff were finding it difficult to understand each other. Programme staff needed support from finance staff; and finance staff needed to be able to understand the needs of the programme and provide appropriate information.

We arranged a series of one-to-one meetings between managers and the finance member of staff dealing with their project. These meetings are held monthly to coincide with the production of budget and actual and donor reports. They usually last less than 30 minutes. In addition, a monthly meeting of all finance and programme staff is held to talk about common concerns. We wonder whether meeting every two months might be enough for these larger meetings. The meetings make it possible to share problems and plan the way forward.

There is now greater mutual understanding. Finance people appreciate how difficult it can be to obtain the necessary paperwork donors require, and they have started to consider whether there are other ways of meeting donors' requirements. Programme people have started to appreciate the difficulties of producing the financial reports required, and some have become experts in finance! We hope to develop the relationship further by arranging field visits for finance staff, and to continue financial training for programme staff.

Source: Cini Asha, India

Write clearly. Documents for non-finance staff should be written simply and avoid using any technical language. It takes time to develop these writing skills, but if you want people to understand what you are saying and act on it, it can make a big difference. Rules for writing in this style are shown in Box 14.

Box 14 How to write clearly

- Plan what you want to say before you write.
- Organize the information into sections.
- Avoid technical words, or at least explain them.
- Use positive rather than negative phrases: write 'The cash/bank book will be much easier to control if it is updated regularly', rather than 'If the cash/bank book is not updated regularly, it can be more difficult to control'.
- Use active rather than passive language: write 'We will complete the cash/ bank book' rather than 'The cash/bank book will be completed'.
- Turn nouns into verbs: write 'Your manager will decide if they will reimburse travel expenses' rather than 'All decisions about the reimbursement of travel expenses are decided by your manager'.
- Remove any unwanted words: 'A new bank account is in the process of being set up for you'.
- Be concise: use no more than15–20 words in each sentence.
- Have only one main idea for each sentence.

Source: Cammack, 2012

Other ways of developing the capacity of finance staff

Interviews and tests. When recruiting staff with specific financial responsibilities, set a test based on the kind of work they will have to do. Candidates for a finance job could be asked to agree the organization's own bank records with the bank statement. The test will be one factor in making the selection. Not doing well in the test will not automatically mean rejecting the candidate. However, if such a person is appointed you will be aware of the need for further training.

'Sector' skills. Finance people may not have worked in a non-commercial organization before. The culture of a non-profit organization may be quite different, and it is important for everyone that they feel settled quickly. Issues such as gender equality and social diversity may be new to them, and they may need training. It is vital that the decisions that finance staff make, for example in budgeting, are in accordance with organizational priorities.

Programme visits. The role of finance people is often limited in scope. Although the organization has an exciting programme of activities, they may never see examples of it. Make sure that there are some opportunities for finance staff to visit the programme. This can increase their understanding of the pressures that programme people face.

Organizational aspects: financial information

Up-to-date and accurate financial information is essential for managing the activities of any group or organization. Organizations with paper-based systems need well-trained finance people to help them to keep good records and produce clear financial reports.

For a computerized organization, hardware and/or software may be an old version, and no longer produce what you need. You will need to assess what is the most appropriate software or accounting package for your use. A number of 'off-the-shelf' packages are available but is important to seek advice before introducing it or changing from an existing one. Speak with other non-profit organizations in your area who have experience, and make sure there is local training and support for the package you propose.

Donors may help you to upgrade and may pay for training staff in a new system. If information is always out of date, it is also worth looking at other factors. For example: are there enough staff to provide the level of service you need? Or is there a 'blockage' that prevents inputting of information?

If the financial system is designed primarily for accountants, others may not understand the information. Financial reports must be 'user-friendly' so that readers can understand them, feel competent to question them, and take the necessary decisions.

See also 'Who needs to build budgeting capacity?' in Chapter 3.

Organizational aspects: organizational culture

The role of the leadership team

Members of the management committee and the leader influence how finance is dealt with across an organization. If it is treated as a low priority ('The finance team are wonderful and deal with everything financial, which leaves me able to concentrate on the programme'), you may lose the positive aspects that financial management can offer an organization and its programme. If managers are saying 'It is not my responsibility and I don't want to get involved' (and possibly 'I don't understand it'), this can lead to a lack of control over financial matters and therefore poorer funding prospects.

An organization that treats finance as a high priority ('We all understand the importance of finance here; the finance team are great, and my responsibility is to be financially informed, which helps me to take better decisions'), there will be a positive impact on people throughout the organization.

The leadership team, and especially the leader, need to give a consistent message that finance is important. Good financial behaviour from the leader must support this message, for example completing a tour expenses form as soon as they return from a trip.

A change in the leadership's message about finance can, very quickly, influence an organization's culture, either positively or negatively. The message about the importance of finance needs to be constantly reinforced.

Story: A leader's influence

Everyone was excited when a new director arrived at a well-run organization. The organization had ten members of staff, most of whom worked with community groups to build their capacity. It had excellent financial and management systems and a number of long-term donors.

The new director had many ideas of how to develop the programme work, and these were introduced with great success. She was, however, not interested in managing the organization; she delegated every responsibility that was not directly related to the programme. She would praise administrative staff for their contribution, and was often heard to say that she did not need to check the finances because 'we have a talented and trustworthy administrator'. This meant that the administrator made financial decisions which should have been made by the director. No one bothered to monitor budgets or check that donor reporting was up to date. Financial controls were not applied, and requests for payments were authorized by senior staff without knowing what they were signing for.

After eighteen months, the organization faced serious problems. First, two long-standing donors withdrew their funding, saying that its financial management was not up to the required standard. Second, the administrator had stolen money from the organization over six months and no one had noticed until the annual external audit. The administrator was dismissed, with a lot of negative publicity. The programme had to be reduced dramatically, and the future of the organization became very uncertain.

Source: training workshops in Asia

Non-finance staff

Non-finance staff often need basic financial management skills to do their job. Programme staff, for example, working with community groups and partners, may be asked to help them to prepare a budget, keep a record of money coming in and going out, operate a bank account, and present a report on what has been spent. Staff in these situations should be able to advise confidently, but also to recognize the limits of their knowledge. You may sometimes need to say 'This is beyond my expertise and I need to ask someone else to help'.

Box 15 lists some questions to ask about the working relationships between programme and finance staff.

Financial training. Training for non-finance people can improve their understanding of financial matters. Sometimes finance people within the organization can provide it; if not, you need to bring in an outside facilitator. Such a training event in itself can raise the profile of finance as well as build the capacity of non-finance staff. (See also 'Training for financial management capacity building', Chapter 12).

Recruitment. When recruiting non-finance staff whose jobs include financial responsibilities, you should include a numerical test, such as comparing a budget and actual statement (similar to Table 1 in Chapter 3) and asking the interviewee to suggest points to follow up.

Box 15 Questions about working relationships between programme and finance staff

- Does the leader give finance a high priority?
- Does the leader complete his/her personal financial returns on time?
- Do finance and programme staff meet regularly to discuss monthly/quarterly budgets and/or donor reports?
- Is financial training available for non-finance staff?
- Do finance staff have opportunities to visit programme activities?
- Are finance staff involved when new programmes are planned?
- Are finance staff encouraged to avoid using jargon when talking to non-finance people?
- Is at least one person able to communicate about finance with non-finance people in a way that they understand?
- Do interviews for programme staff dealing with financial work include a practical numerical test?
- Do chairs of meetings regularly ask 'What are the financial implications of this decision?'
- Are finance staff given opportunities to contribute effectively to the organization's objectives?
- Where is the location of offices and desks of the finance and programme staff in relation to each other?

Organizational aspects: external relationships

Organizations need to relate well to a range of 'stakeholders': groups and individuals, internal or external, who have an interest in the organization's well-being. They include:

- community groups and partner organizations;
- key donors and other funders;
- other groups operating in each community, for example religious organizations and other non-profit organizations;
- paid staff and volunteers;
- suppliers of goods and services, banks and auditors;
- local and national government.

Key financial relationships exist with the first two of these stakeholders: communities and partners, and donors.

Communities and partners

It is important to inform your communities and/or partners about the financial position of your organization. Tell them what it means for the priorities of their community. This will help to increase their participation in the activities that you are running, which may strengthen the impact of the programme.

Find appropriate ways of explaining how you plan to use money that you have allocated to them, and later how you actually used it (Cammack, 2012). For example:

- Use paper or a whiteboard to present the key areas of your budget linked to the objectives.
- Use visual presentations. Include a bar chart or pie diagram in a programme newsletter to show where the money has come from and where it has gone to. Computer spreadsheet programs can easily convert figures into diagrams.
- Draw a poster with similar details that can be displayed where members of the community and service users gather.
- Give out printed copies of financial information, summarized on no more than one page, following the good practice in communicating financial information. See Box 13.

- Call a meeting to discuss financial priorities, plans and reports, explaining what they mean for their community; invite a skilled communicator who understands finance.
- Use meetings to present audit findings.
- Provide opportunities for feedback and questions.
- Translate materials into the language(s) used.

Make sure that women and poorer members of the community are not left out of the discussions. If you are working in a community where gender issues are very sensitive, you may, for example, need to find ways of reaching the female members of the community by perhaps using a female facilitator.

If you are working with partners, their financial management capacity can be linked to yours. Funding is often given as part of a chain. Reporting back from one partner to another must be done well. The original donor is more likely to continue funding if you submit adequate financial reports. Many of the ideas in this book can be applied to organizations of any size to help build each other's capacity. Share them with your partner organizations.

Donors

Many organizations rely on external funding to continue their programme. One aspect of building financial management capacity is to have a strong relationship with donors. You need to have a commitment from them to fund your programme over several years, if possible. Donors can in practice be a catalyst for building your capacity, by demanding a high standard of financial reporting and providing financial management capacity-building inputs.

This usually means an organization must comply with the requirements of donors for accurate and up-to-date reports, and strong financial systems. But donors are sometimes willing to help organizations that find this challenging. These donor inputs may include an invitation to attend financial training workshops that the donor provides, or funds; on-the-job training for finance staff; funds for external audits; and advice about the kinds of system that might be appropriate.

What could go wrong?

However well an organization is running, it is necessary to consider what could go wrong. This is often part of longer-term planning. Larger organizations sometimes call this 'planning for risks'. These include the withdrawal of donor funding, political changes, or new national legislation. Risks may be external and out of your control, or internal, for example key staff (paid or voluntary) leaving without warning. Larger organizations often have formal risk policies, but all organizations must ask the following questions:

- What could go wrong?
- How likely is it to happen?
- What impact would it have?
- What would we do if it happened?
- What can we do to prevent it?
- Would any of these events mean that we could not continue?

Asking the questions and thinking about the consequences helps to protect an organization from the many uncertainties that they face. The management committee and staff need to discuss these issues at least once each year.

What are 'risks'?

'A risk is a potentially damaging outcome of an event or situation, which could be internal or external to the organization. It could have major or minor effects, or it could have none. A responsible organization anticipates the risks involved in its work, makes well-considered decisions on how to address them, and ensures that it acts on those decisions to protect the people who could be put at risk and the organization itself.'

Source: Clark, 2001

Extra questions about financial sustainability

Figure 2 in Chapter 2 ('Aspects of strong financial management capacity') shows the specific tasks and organizational aspects of building capacity. However, there are a number of other important questions to ask that have wider financial implications for how an organization is managed, as it moves towards financial sustainability:

- Is there clear longer-term planning which includes financing plans?
- Has the organization thought through how it funds non-programme (or 'core') costs?
- Has the management committee considered the need for organizational savings (also called 'reserves') and does it have a 'reserves policy'?

We will consider each of these questions in Part Three, 'Moving towards sustainability'.

Box 16 Organizational aspects of financial management – common concerns

Concerns	*Possible solutions*
We are a rural organization with no access to professional accounting skills. We are not able to use computers very often.	First decide what accounting records and reports you need, by talking with donors and stakeholders. Some organizations only need paper-based basic accounting. Systems can usually be designed to provide what you need with the skills and resources that you have, perhaps with some outside help from time to time.
No one is responsible for finance at the meetings of our management committee. They don't think they need anyone.	Someone must prioritize the financial side of the work. Convince members of the importance of this. Suggest someone joins the committee who is willing to take on the role, or suggest one of the existing members.
Only the finance person on our management committee understands our budget and actual reports.	Improve the clarity of the information given to the management committee. Train members to interpret the information and ask questions.
Are we large enough to have a finance sub-committee?	If there is not enough time to deal with financial issues at the meetings of the management committee, it could be useful to appoint a finance sub-committee which would have more time to go into details. However, don't let this be a reason for not discussing finance at the main management committee meetings. All its members are still responsible.
Accountants are expensive and hard to recruit. We are a small organization and can't afford someone with the right qualifications.	Decide how much financial information you need to produce and whether you need a professional accountant. If so, divide the work between routine tasks and professional work. Think about a part-time person for the professional work, and see if you can absorb the routine tasks into other jobs. Consider recruiting someone at a junior level and supporting them through professional training.

Concerns	Possible solutions
I can't understand our finance manager. He talks in jargon.	A two-way approach is needed. You need to find help in understanding some of the jargon; the finance manager needs help to communicate better. Start by sharing the advice in Boxes 13 and 15.
Our finance staff say that the software we are using is not suitable for what we need, but we can't afford anything better.	Talk with other non-profit organizations and donors about the possibilities. Donors may be willing to fund new software. Don't forget to add to the budget the cost of training staff to use the software. Old software that cannot give up-to-date and 'user-friendly' financial information can also be expensive in staff time and lead to poorly managed programmes.
Our leader doesn't understand financial issues and covers it up by getting other people to do everything.	Leaders must have a working knowledge of finance and understand its importance. Confidential financial management tutoring (see pages 138–9) for the leader from an outside facilitator may help them to develop without 'losing face'.
Programme staff are often asked for financial advice, but don't feel confident to give it.	Arrange some training in basic financial management for staff. Either find a suitable course for non-profit organiza-tions; or, if possible, arrange your own training. Use your finance people, or ask an outside facilitator to help. Put the cost of this in your next budget. Some donors would be willing to fund this.
Our management committee only look at current issues, never at the future.	Arrange a special meeting to consider longer-term issues. Start by thinking about possible 'risks' and ways to deal with them.

PART THREE

Moving towards sustainability

CHAPTER 9

Organizational sustainability, planning and core costs

In earlier chapters we have considered the skills, systems, and organizational factors needed to build financial management capacity. This chapter looks at how longer-term planning and financing plans move an organization towards sustainability. A part of this is how to finance non-programme or 'core' costs.

Keywords: longer-term/strategic planning; financing plans; funding mix; core costs; financial sustainability; role of finance people in managing core costs

The three elements, **longer-term planning, financing plans**, and **core costs** appear in Figure 3; the fourth element of the financial sustainability jigsaw, **organizational savings** (or 'reserves'), is discussed in Chapter 10.

Organizational 'sustainability' is sometimes seen as the ultimate aim for a non-profit organization. Some non-profits are started with a specific objective and not intended to exist for more than a limited time period. Others can be a key part of the community.

Non-profit organizations sometimes say that their aim is 'not to be needed any more'. This may be true in the long term, but in the short term communities and service users may rely on them for their day-to-day existence. Non-profit organizations must therefore make every effort to become financially sustainable if they are to continue.

http://dx.doi.org/10.3362/9781780448244.003

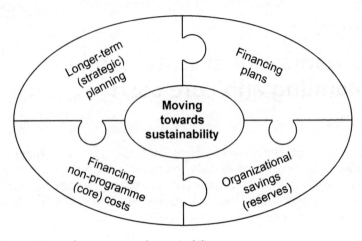

Figure 3 Ways of moving towards sustainability

Building financial management capacity, in the way described in Part Two of this book, is the first stage of becoming sustainable. The four pieces of the jigsaw in Figure 3 then move an organization closer towards sustainability. Every organization is different, so building capacity and sustainability means planning for your own situation.

Moving toward sustainability: longer-term planning

Longer-term planning is also called 'strategic planning'. In small groups this may be simply to answer the question 'what do we want to achieve over the next few years and how do we do it?' In larger organizations it can be a process, involving senior managers, management board members and other stakeholders, which considers the current situation, its objectives for the future, and how these might be achieved.

> **What is 'strategic planning'?**
>
> 'A systematic process through which an organization agrees on its priorities and builds commitment to them among its key stakeholders. These priorities are selected as the most effective way of fulfilling the organization's mission, taking account of its changing operating environment'.
>
> *Source*: Methodist Relief and Development Fund, 2011

Benefits of strategic planning

The benefits of strategic planning are not only financial. Most relate directly to programme and other activities of the organization. Improved programme impact resulting from longer-term planning will attract better funding and make you more financially sustainable too.

Other benefits are:

- highlighting organizational purpose, goals, values and priorities;
- identifying organizational strengths and longer-term objectives;
- making clear to communities, partners, staff and volunteers what you want to achieve;
- motivating and keeping the commitment of stakeholders;
- showing donors what you plan to do, and that you are taking longer-term planning seriously.

Strategic planning helps an organization focus on its priorities, make full use of its resources, and communicate its decisions. It makes sure that decisions are based on helping the organization to achieve the things it wants to do. It is usually done every few years, for a period of between three and five years. Decide an appropriate time period for your organization.

A full description of strategic planning is outside the scope of this book. Details of further resources are in the 'Written resources' and 'Web resources' at the end of this book.

Moving toward sustainability: financing plans

Financing plans are part of the broader strategic planning process, and are usually prepared at the same time. The strategic plan's objectives will decide what programme activities are needed, and whether they are sustainable in terms of staffing and organizational capacity. The financial plan must then consider how these objectives will be financed.

Many organizations complete a budget (see Chapter 3), but financing plans are different. Budgets consider the income and expenditure for the next year; financing plans look at broader issues, for example where the income will come from over the next five years. It looks at all types of financing, not just donor funding. The plan may also result in the preparation of an outline budget for coming years, but this is not the primary purpose of the plan.

Preparing a financing plan

The plan draws on the objectives in the strategic plan. It considers the strengths and weaknesses of the organization, the context it is operating in, and what might go wrong. The activities to deliver these objectives help determine the amount of money needed. The financing plan decides what is possible within future financing constraints. If the plan shows that enough money cannot be raised, then the activities will need reducing, or other income sources found.

There are three stages in preparing the financing plan:

Analyse your current situation. Think realistically about your current financial situation: how you finance your programme activities, and what stops you doing more. You may wish to undertake a strengths, weaknesses, opportunities and threats (SWOT) analysis to assess your current financial situation (see Figure 4).

In considering your strengths, weaknesses, opportunities and threats, a SWOT analysis is a practical way of assessing either a whole organization, or a part of the organization (for example its current financial situation). The information can then be used to decide how to build on strengths and opportunities, and minimize weaknesses and threats.

Figure 4 SWOT Analysis

	Positive	Negative
Internal	**Strengths** What do we do well? How do we build on our strengths?	**Weaknesses** What do we not do well? How could we reduce the weaknesses?
External	**Opportunities** What opportunities do we have? How do we make the most of these opportunities?	**Threats** What threats are we vulnerable to? How can we avoid possible threats?

Ask and answer questions such as: What is our current financial position? Have we had a surplus or deficit in recent years? Where is our income coming from? How dependent are we on donor funding? How reliable is our funding? Do we rely on only one or two funders? What income is guaranteed for future years and what may stop? How much income is specified for a particular purpose and how much of the rest can we decide how to use? What demand is there for the services we provide? How do we fund non-programme costs? How much do we have in organizational savings?

Decide what you want to achieve. Think about where you want to be financially in three to five years' time. Allow time to think through the possibilities as if you had no limitations on what you could achieve, before you decide what is realistic. Be bold in your thinking!

Ask and answer questions such as: What resources do we need to achieve all our objectives? What existing commitments do we want/need to stop? How will we replace existing funds that are for a limited period? What is the future demand for the services we provide? How will their costs increase in future years? How much do we want in funds specified for a particular purpose and how much of the rest do we want to decide how to use? What balance do we want between funding from donors and other sources? (sometimes called the 'funding mix', see page 111). How do we want to fund our non-programme costs? How much do we want to have in organizational savings?

We will consider these last three questions in more detail in this and the next chapter.

Plan how you will get there. This section allows you to consider 'your current situation' and 'what you want to achieve', and to plan how you move from one to the other.

Ask and answer questions such as: What resources are available now? How can we move towards the right mix of funding for us? What additional resources are needed to do this? What longer-term items do we need to fund? (for example, computers, vehicles, equipment). How will we fund programme activities and non-programme costs? How can we increase the amount of income not tied to any particular activity? What will be our charging policy (if you charge service users)? How can we increase our organizational savings? Who will we accept money from? When is it right for us to say 'no' to donors? What could go wrong and how can we prepare for this? What situations could happen and how would we deal with them?

Having planned these three stages, and when the organization and its stakeholders have agreed them, you are ready to go to the next stage.

How will we implement and monitor the financing plan?

Now your planning moves into action. New activities will start and existing ones may end. You will need to include the objectives of the plan in annual budgets, and work plans for staff and volunteers. Use them when working with other stakeholders.

The financing plan is likely to change over time. Use measurable outcomes to see how close you are to the plan; for example, set a target amount of donor funding as a proportion of total funding.

Monitor the plan against such outcomes every few months, formally at staff and/or management committee meetings, and informally in conversations with communities, partners, service users and donors. Recognize changes as they happen and update the plan.

The funding mix

What is the 'funding mix'?

The balance between an organization's sources of finance, which help to diversify its income and make it more sustainable.

Many non-profit organizations rely on external funding to continue, but making a financing plan allows you to review what the organization needs and whether other sources of income are possible. Developing the financing plan is the time to consider the right funding mix for your organization. Sometimes this means changing the way your organization thinks about funding.

Relying on external funding alone can be difficult because donors may:

- change their mind and/or limit the period they are willing to support you;
- ask you to follow their plans and priorities rather than your own;
- not fund certain non-programme costs so you have to fund them yourself.

There are three main methods of financing non-profit organizations.

1. Self-financing. This includes:

- **Income from the organization:** membership fees, interest from savings invested.

- **Sales of goods or services:** sales of publications, running conferences, charging for services, contracts with others paying for your services, expert staff acting as consultants, charging others for attending your training courses, renting out part of the premises you own.
- **Income-generating activities:** many activities can be started; for example, workshops created to make and sell crafts and clothes, or repair vehicles. Sometimes selling goods or services can generate income and also fulfil the organization's aims and objectives.

Income generation needs to be carefully managed. Sometimes non-profit organizations may not have the right experience and business skills to start semi-commercial activities. There may also be legal/tax restrictions on whether a non-profit organization is allowed to undertake profit-making activities. In the right circumstances it can be beneficial, but it needs to be well managed to avoid potential losses and/or using up valuable staff time.

2. Local fundraising. This includes:

- **Fundraising from the public:** one-off events, collections, regular giving, special appeals.
- **Appeals to local businesses:** donations, in-kind support, sponsorship of an event.
- **Appeals to local organizations:** religious organizations, trade unions, schools, co-operative and other groups.

Local fundraising sometimes allows you to claim tax benefits and it is worth looking at the possibilities.

The advantage of both *self-financing* and *local fundraising* is that the money can be used as the organization chooses, perhaps to help cover core costs and/or build up reserves (see Chapter 10).

3. External funding. This includes:

- **Local and national government:** grants, joint activities.
- **Local and national non-government organizations (NGOs):** support for specific activities, organizational, and capacity building.
- **International government:** support from international governments mostly channelled through an NGO in their own country.
- **International NGOs:** support for specific activities, organizational, and capacity building.
- **National and international trusts and foundations:** support for specific projects.
- **International embassies:** often small grants.
- **Business sector:** some larger business will provide grants to non-profit organizations.

Whatever 'mix' is right for your organization, the financing plan will be the starting point to think through the possibilities.

Moving toward sustainability: financing non-programme core costs

What are core costs?

Non-programme organizational costs including rent, office costs, and the salaries of administrative staff. Core costs are sometimes called 'administrative costs', 'indirect costs', 'overheads' or 'support costs'.

External donors may be unwilling to fund core costs, preferring to contribute to programme costs instead. However, the full cost of providing a programme includes the costs of the programme itself plus a proportion of core costs. If core costs are not covered, the organization cannot be effective or financially sustainable and cannot plan for its future, or even continue. It is therefore important to find ways of covering these costs – but this is not easy.

Core costs do not always increase in line with extra activities. For example, smaller organizations with one or two programme activities may have a relatively high level of core costs; organizations with twenty activities may be better able to spread their costs and achieve some 'economies of scale'. The cost of a vehicle is the same for all organizations, but for a smaller organization it is a larger proportion of its costs.

The management committee are responsible for making sure that there is a plan to fund the core costs for future years.

Different stages of development

Organizations with only one activity, and one donor, may already include all their core costs in their budget and be fully funded. But financing core costs is more difficult for organizations that have more than one activity, several donors, and expenses which the budgeting and accounting do not directly link to their programme activities.

Drawing on Mike Hudson's research, Bill Bruty (2005) identifies three stages of organizational development.

Infancy. This is where organizations are heavily dependent on a single financing source, and growth is limited by their donor's capacity to provide more funding. Relying on one donor could limit the organization's independence.

Growth phase. As the organization grows and becomes more independent, there is a danger of being pulled in different directions by new donors. This may not fit organizational objectives. To balance this, the organization should aim to keep its original donors, attract a mix of new donors, and, if it can, develop its own fundraising.

Maturity and maintenance. At this stage, financing should come from a changing mix of sources, to give the organization greater security of income. A lack of accountability to donors can cause complacency in mature organizations and lead to possible decline.

Ways to finance core costs

There are a number of options. Some of the options are shown in the 'The funding mix' section (pages 109–11), but those relating to core costs are summarized below.

Using the 'administration allowance' from donors. Some donors are willing to add an administrative allowance (perhaps between 5 and 20 per cent) to a grant for programme work. This is intended to cover core costs, although smaller amounts are often not enough. It is worth finding out exactly what the allowance is supposed to cover, and if it is possible to include any other administrative costs elsewhere in the programme budget.

Reducing core costs to a minimum. Non-profit organizations usually run on minimum core costs, but it is worth looking at your costs and seeing if you can do the same work for less money: for example, whether there is a cheaper alternative for maintaining your computers. Use of volunteers and in-kind support can help to reduce costs considerably. An occasional reminder to staff/volunteers to minimize travel, photocopying, and telephone calls might also be helpful.

Using your own funds and raising funds locally. Some organizations have 'unrestricted' funds that they can use, perhaps derived from membership fees or charges for services. It may also be possible to use existing activities as a source of income. See 'The funding mix' section for possible ways. You might, for example, offer training courses to outsiders, charging them a fee and so recovering the costs of the course. It is important to manage this kind of fundraising well, making sure that the full cost (including staff time) is not bigger than the income generated. Any proposed activities should be in line with the organization's overall objectives and not divert staff from their main work.

Finding a donor that covers core costs. These donors are unusual, and you are fortunate if you find one. Funding core costs (alone) is sometimes offered for newer organizations to help them to develop their organizational capacity. It is sometimes described as an 'organization building' grant.

Allocating core costs to programme activity budgets. A proportion of core costs is allocated to the programme budgets (see below).

Accounting options

The last of the options shown above ('allocating core costs') can make a big difference to an organization's financing, but it requires more accounting work to achieve it. Larger organizations often employ accountants and fundraisers to maximize their income by including core costs with programme budgets, but smaller organizations with more than one programme activity may also consider this.

Full cost of activities. It is important for leaders and managers to know the full cost of an activity. This will include activity costs (for example salaries, travel) plus hidden costs that are not charged to the activity, for example some core costs. You need to ask 'what proportion of core costs (if any) relates to this activity?' If some of the costs are charged to a central budget, then it really is an activity cost, and should possibly be funded by the donor. Also ask 'are some staff's salaries paid for as core costs even though they are working part-time on the activity?' For example the finance person may be spending a proportion of their time accounting and reporting for the activity. Where is this expense budgeted and accounted for?

Allocating core costs to programme activity budgets. Your core costs could be allocated to each activity budget. If you have five activities of an equal size, you could, for example, charge one fifth of the office costs to each. This would move these costs away from your core-costs budget and include them in the budgets for your activities, if it could be justified. You might argue, for example, that the office costs would not be needed unless you had this programme of activities.

You could take the same approach with a leader's salary, if he or she is spending time with each of the five different activities. A proportion of the salary costs could be allocated to each, in proportion to the time spent. It is not usually necessary for people to keep time sheets or detailed records to determine the exact hours, although a few donors insist on this. Instead, an annual estimation of time spent on each activity is made and, as long as it can be justified, it is often acceptable.

If you allocate core costs to activity budgets, three things happen.

- **You see the full activity cost:** your organization can take decisions based on what a programme is really costing. For example, whether this is the best use of your resources, or if you could do the same work for less.
- **You control costs better:** staff or volunteers are familiar with what everything is costing in their activity, and whether they need to reduce spending.
- **You encourage 'full-cost' funding from some donors:** presenting the full cost of an activity to a donor means that they are more likely to fund it and help you to recover your core costs.

This approach is sometimes called 'full-cost recovery', or 'activity-based costing'. Detailed methods for recovering core costs are outside the scope of this book but, if you need advice, you will find resources suggested in the 'Web resources' and 'Written resources' sections at the end of this book.

If you do allocate core costs to the programme activities, remember that donors will not cover these if they are already giving you an 'administration allowance'. Most organizations aim for a mixture of the different methods to cover their core costs. This needs careful accounting to maximize the available funding and avoid any possible double counting.

Story: Allocating core costs to programme budgets

Projekta is a non-profit NGO founded in 1993. We focus on building capacity in the areas of gender equality and governance.

Ensuring financial stability and funding our core costs are a major challenge. From the beginning, we have divided costs into two types: those related to the implementation of the programme activities, sometimes called 'direct costs'; and those related to core costs. The core costs were treated separately in the budget, because Projekta received financial support from a Dutch agency specifically to cover the cost of running the office.

Dividing the budget into two parts, however, meant that we did not know how much each programme was costing us, or how strong or weak we were in financial terms. We did not even know whether Projekta would be able to continue its work if the Dutch funding ended.

A few years ago, we decided to introduce 'activity-based costing' into our budgeting and accounting. This tries to combine both programme costs and core costs. When we prepare the annual budget, we estimate the total core costs and divide them between the programmes, in proportion to staff hours worked on each programme.

The programme budgets that we offer to donors then show all their costs. If donors give us a fixed percentage of the proposed budget to help to cover administrative costs, we put it into a budget line from which we pay charges for rent, telephone, and transportation, plus core staff salaries – in fact all costs not directly relating to programme activities.

Even if a donor is not willing to contribute towards covering core costs, we still go ahead with the programme. We rely on our own fundraising, sometimes by taking on an external consultancy which brings in money and contributes towards the missing amount of core costs.

Activity-based costing gives us better information on the full cost of each programme and helps us to fund them all. Most importantly, we can keep control of our costs. If they are too high, it alerts us to look for cheaper alternatives.

Source: Stichting Projekta, Surinam

The role of finance people

You cannot assume that all finance people know how to fund core costs. This is a management issue rather than a financial issue, and someone in the leadership team may have to suggest the options. Most trained book-keepers and professional accountants will understand the principle of how to allocate core costs to programme budgets. The way in which you then present this information to donors is vital, and it is important that your finance people and those responsible for fundraising work together. Seek professional advice about core-costs accounting, if you need it.

Box 17 Sustainability, planning and core costs – common concerns

Concerns	_Possible solutions_
We are a small group of volunteers and wonder whether we need to put together a longer-term plan.	Although small, it is worth thinking through what you want to achieve longer term, and how it might be financed. Involve your group in deciding what are your strengths, and identifying objectives for the next few years and how they might be achieved.
We are a medium-sized organization with staff and premises and communities who rely on us for support. We think we need a financing plan but don't know where to start.	Use the information in this chapter for the financing plan: analyse your current position, decide where you want to be, and how you will get there. Involve your stakeholders in thinking about the possibilities and write down your plan.
We only receive funding from one donor. We do not need to prepare a financing plan.	If your funding is from one donor and they decide not to continue, the organization may need to close. If you need to be sustainable and continue longer-term, think about the other financing options in this chapter. Sometimes a donor will help you think this through and provide ideas.
None of our donors will fund core costs.	Make sure that any core costs which directly relate to a programme are budgeted and charged to that programme. Look for donors who will at least add an 'administration' percentage towards your core costs. Ask the leadership team to decide how to fund these costs, considering the five ways shown earlier in this chapter.

Concerns	Possible solutions
Our donors already give a percentage for 'administration', so they will not cover any other core costs.	Talk with your donors to find out exactly what the administration percentage covers. Consider all your costs carefully and make sure your split between 'programme' and 'core costs' is accurate. See if any of your 'core costs' relate directly to the programme. For example, telephone costs may be charged to core costs in the budget, but in reality many of the calls, and a proportion of the rental charge, benefit the programme directly. Add in any costs to the programme budget that the administration percentage does not cover.
All our funding is restricted. Although our donors give us an 'administration allowance', it is not enough to fund our core costs.	See if any of your costs can be reduced and whether you could raise any 'unrestricted' funds yourself, to help to fund the difference.
Our donor wants to know why we have included some core costs in the programme budget.	Tell the donor that you have included the full cost of the activity in the programme budget. This includes a proportion of the costs of running the organization. Explain how your organization works, and that it only exists to provide its activities (if this is true). If there were no activities, you would not need any core costs.

CHAPTER 10

Moving towards sustainability: reserves

This chapter explains what reserves are, whether your organization needs them, how to calculate an appropriate level, and practical ways of building them up. It also considers the use of a 'reserves policy' and explains how thinking about reserves may make a useful contribution to making your organization sustainable in the long term.

Keywords: organizational savings; reserves; appropriate level of reserves; reserves policy; restricted and unrestricted funds; designated funds; endowment funds

Many non-profit organizations need donors to fund their work so that they can continue their activities. If, however, there is not enough financing for a particular year, an organization can sometimes use some of its savings – or 'reserves' – from previous years.

Reserve funds are the 'unrestricted' money (that is not allocated to a specific programme), over and above the money that an organization receives and spends in a particular year. They can be seen as 'organizational savings'. Reserves are 'that part of a charity's income funds that is freely available' (Charity Commission, 2008). Some organizations describe reserves as 'funds' (see Box 18). They act as a safety net in case income suddenly drops or expenditure increases.

Story: What are 'reserves'?

A personal story
In my first year of work I received a salary of 10,500. My expenses for rent, travel to work, food, and entertainment cost me 9,750. I put 750 into my savings account.

The second year I again received 10,500 as salary, but in addition to my expenses of 9,750 I had to pay health costs of a further 1,000 – a total of 10,750. I took the extra 250 that I needed from my savings. It left 500 in my savings account.

An organization's story
In the first year we started, we had 10,500 from donations. Our project expenses, travel, newsletter production, and meetings came to 9,750. We put 750 into our savings account.

The second year we again received 10,500 and paid our expenses of 9,750; but this year we also had a new health project costing 1,000 more – a total of 10,750. We took the extra 250 from our savings account. We were still able to keep 500 in our savings account. We started to call the money in our savings account our 'reserves'. We do not need it yet, but we may do in future years.

Source: training workshop, Lebanon

Box 18 Different types of fund

Restricted funds ('earmarked', 'tied' or 'ring-fenced')
Money given by a donor for a particular purpose. The funds can only be used for that purpose. They cannot be used to create a reserve fund.

Unrestricted funds ('free money' or 'general purpose income')
Money given by a donor for general use or raised by the organization itself, for example through membership fees or fundraising.

Designated funds
Unrestricted money that the management committee has set aside for a particular purpose, for example for repairs to premises in a future year. The management committee must 'designate' these funds for this purpose. They can be 'undesignated' later, but only by the management committee.

Endowment funds (or 'corpus funds')
Money given by a donor (or sometimes saved from previous years' surpluses) that the organization invests in order to provide interest for running costs. 'Permanent' endowments allow only the interest of the fund to be used, not the fund itself. 'Expendable' endowments are funds that the management committee can either invest or convert into income. These funds can be either restricted or unrestricted, depending on the donor.

General funds (or 'income and expenditure account')
Money still held from the current year and previous years' surpluses.

Do you need to worry about reserves?

Some organizations have no reserves and spend all that they receive, each year. Some find that building up reserves is impossible, because they rarely receive unrestricted funds and it is difficult to raise more funds. Some do not really need to hold reserves: groups or organizations with no paid staff, premises, or ongoing commitments can manage without additional money to act as their 'safety net'. If they run out of money, they either stop working, or pay for what they need themselves.

In countries where there is a medium to high inflation rate, holding money in the bank does not help an organization, because inflation can absorb the savings that have been put aside as reserves. Also, in some countries banks do not pay interest on deposited money. In such countries, if the law allows, surplus unrestricted money is sometimes used to purchase items that will not decrease in value, for example a building whose rent is used as income for the organization. If this is not possible, organizations usually do not keep bank or cash reserves.

However, in most countries organizations with paid staff, premises, and commitments to communities and/or partners must hold some reserves. As an organization grows, it needs to consider whether it would be able to continue if some or all of its financing stopped, and whether it is essential that its services continue to be provided. If so, the organization needs reserves.

Why hold reserves?

Reserves are held for several purposes:

- to provide for times when money due is received after money paid;
- to allow work to continue if income/fund-raising is not as high as expected;
- to provide time to make savings or raise funds if money expected is not received or is received late;
- to be able to spend money that has not been planned or budgeted for, if an opportunity or emergency arises.

It is important to find out what is actually included as reserves. The savings built up over previous years may, for example, be in the bank account. However, bank balances may still not be available to spend if donors have given them for a particular purpose and will only allow them to be spent on that. Or if savings are invested in a building or equipment, this money too may not be readily available to spend.

The level of reserves

It can be difficult to decide the level of reserves that an organization needs. For example, donors may not give funds if they think that an organization is holding too much money in reserve. But if too little is held, the management committee may be putting the organization's sustainability at risk and donors may feel that funding them is not a good use of their money.

Each organization has different needs, and the level of reserves will depend on its type and size. For example, a small organization with few staff and secure financing may need only low reserves. A larger organization offering an ever changing range of services, which has a large staff and which finds it difficult to get enough financing each year, needs higher reserves. A list of factors to consider when deciding on the level of reserves to hold is shown in Box 19.

Box 19 Factors to consider when deciding the level of reserves

- whether you are required by law or by donors to hold reserves at a particular level;
- the effect on communities and/or partners if you were unable to provide the services;
- the range and reliability of income sources;
- the proportions of 'restricted' and 'unrestricted' income;
- current and expected future plans and levels of expenditure;
- the sensitivity of income and expenditure to outside influences, for example government rules;
- the value of outstanding commitments;
- the level at which reserves may discourage donors from providing further funding;
- whether the current reserves are in bank or cash, or invested in buildings and equipment;
- the size of any investments;
- your ability to respond quickly to changing circumstances, and the time it would take to raise more funds;
- the amount of 'unrestricted' money that is raised through any membership fees, donations, and local fundraising.

Reserves policy

For organizations which have regular commitments, employ staff, and have their own offices, it is good practice to produce a written policy on reserves. It should include the following items:

- the reason for keeping reserves;
- the level of reserves needed;
- how this level will be achieved/maintained;
- how often the policy is reviewed.

Reserves policies are often expressed as either a proportion of income or a proportion of expenditure. They could also be expressed as a time period, for example '50 per cent or six months of budgeted expenditure'. This means that if all financing stopped, the reserves would be enough to pay for activities for a further six months. This would provide time for more fundraising or an orderly reduction in activities. Policies are usually reviewed annually, or at least every few years. An example of a reserves policy is shown in Box 20.

Box 20 Example of a reserves policy

Santé needs to keep reserves to cover changes in fundraising and so that we can continue to provide ongoing services to our service users and the communities with which we work. We aim to hold reserves at 35%, or just over four months, of our expenditure budget. This target should be achieved over the next three years. It will be in place by 31 December 20--. The management committee will then review this percentage annually when the budget is being set.

The policy may be drafted by a member of staff, or an organization's auditor, or a professional accountant, but it is the management committee's responsibility to approve it and make sure that it is in place. The policy should be included in the annual report and accounts, thereby demonstrating that the organization is acting openly in justifying the level of reserves to its stakeholders.

Perhaps the main benefit of having a policy is to allow those responsible to think through and plan how they would keep the organization going if they could not raise enough funds. Planning for an appropriate level of reserves, even if it is not achievable immediately, shows that you are managing your organization in a responsible way and it is a contribution towards making the organization sustainable.

Story: A reserves policy

The Centre for the Study of Violence and Reconciliation was founded in 1989.

We were concerned that the Centre did not have a policy on reserves, and the money that it did hold could give donors the impression that it did not need their funding. A policy would explain to funders and supporters why it was necessary for the Centre to hold money, rather than spend it all, even though the reserves were only to be used for times when there were delays in receiving grants or funding was short.

We felt that writing a policy would help us to plan better, would support the fundraising effort, and would improve the allocation of resources. The reserves would have to be built up over a period, for example from surplus unrestricted funds or from income-generating projects.

We needed the level of reserves to be high enough to allow us to deal with temporary downturns in fundraising without having to reduce programme expenditure. We knew that some organizations calculate reserves as being three months of either salaries or total operating expenditure. We calculated both. In the end we were recommended to base the amount on three months' operating costs and to build up to this gradually. Any interest from the reserves held would contribute towards our running costs.

The policy will be approved by the board and published in the Centre's procedures manual and annual financial statements and report. Once established, the policy and the amount will be reviewed regularly, at least every three years.

Source: Centre for the Study of Violence and Reconciliation, South Africa

Methods of building up reserves

It can be difficult to build up reserves. Here are two suggestions:

- *Talk with your donor.* Some donors will say they will not fund reserves; if so, accept their decision and move on. Other donors understand the issue, will discuss your policy with you, and may make helpful suggestions. It is certainly acceptable to approach donors. Some organizations feel embarrassed to ask – don't be! Some donors see organizations that have low reserves or no reserves as a bad risk for their funding.
- *Build up a surplus of unrestricted funds gradually.* Increase reserves to the necessary level by using some 'unrestricted' funds each year – even if only a small amount. This may

involve using money from local fundraising events, membership fees, charges for services, small donations, or income-generating projects. See other ideas in 'The funding mix', Chapter 9, pages 109–11. It may take several years to reach the level that you need, and it should be seen as an organizational objective and part of the budget-planning process.

Changes in reserves and the budget

If reserves are to be either created or increased, the income part of the budget should be greater than the expenditure for that year.

Total income	100,000
Total expenditure	98,000
Contribution to reserves	**2,000**

However, including the figures in the budget does not necessarily mean that it will happen. The management committee must regularly monitor the budget to make sure that expenditure is kept within the set limit, and that all expected income is received.

A 'deficit budget' will use up some of the existing reserves. This should be planned in advance, but only if you have some reserves to spare.

Total income	98,000
Total expenditure	100,000
Reduction in reserves	**2,000**

Box 21 Reserves – common concerns

Concerns	Possible solutions
We are a small voluntary organization with no staff or other commitments. We raise our own funds and spend what we raise each year. Do we need reserves?	Probably not. Keep a small amount in your bank account in case you want to pay out an amount before you raise the funds. If you grow in size, or receive donor funding, think about reserves again.
Our organization has never thought about reserves, but the communities we work with would find it very difficult if we stopped operating.	It is worth looking at ways to build reserves, if not immediately then in the longer term. Discuss it with the management committee and decide how much would be needed to make the organization sustainable. Think of ways to raise this amount.
All our funding is for a particular purpose, and we cannot build up any reserves from it.	Discuss whether it is important for you to have reserves. If so, decide whether you can raise your own funds, maybe through local fundraising, or a minimal charge for services, or membership fees. Talk with your donor about the possibilities.
We have reserves, but no reserves policy.	A policy is useful to explain to donors that you have thought about the issue and are managing your organization in a professional way. Write out a draft policy, ask your management committee to discuss and approve it, and then publish it with your annual accounting statements.

PART FOUR

Tools for building financial management capacity

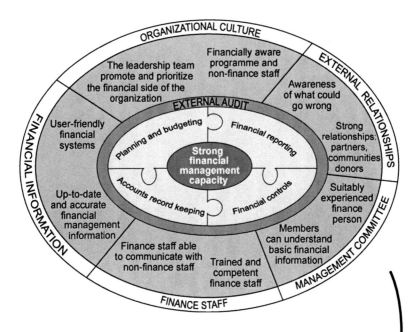

Putting it all together

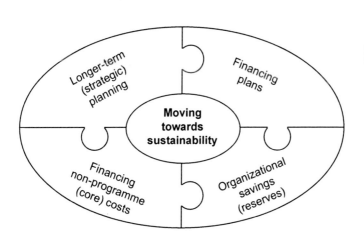

CHAPTER 11

Toolkit for financial management capacity building

Earlier chapters have considered a number of areas in which to build financial management capacity, and now we turn to possible ways to put the ideas into practice. This chapter provides a toolkit of methods that have been used elsewhere and have been found to work well to build financial capacity.

Keywords: financial management capacity building; developing non-profit finance and programme relationship; building leadership's financial management capacity; building financial management capacity of finance and non-finance people; building financial management resource capacity

Capacity building can often be a slow and messy process. Many organizations want a 'quick fix' – maybe a single training course – but it is rarely quite so easy. Every organization is different, and your needs are probably unique. Your capacity-building needs must be fully understood, and then 'tailor-made' to suit your organization. Often a mixture of methods is needed.

Talk to staff and volunteers from other organizations and to your stakeholders, to find out what might be possible. Donors will often bring suggestions from other organizations that they know and will sometimes provide funding for initiatives too. Most donors agree that capacity building is an excellent idea, but some are less willing to help you to put it into practice. If you can, work with donors who can help you to achieve what you want. Don't be afraid to state your needs clearly. If you need help to build capacity, consider

http://dx.doi.org/10.3362/9781780448244.004

bringing in people with the right skills from outside your organization.

This 'toolkit' is offered for use with your group or organization and others that you know. All of the approaches described below have already worked well elsewhere. You might want to use all of them, or none. That's fine. Use methods that work best in your situation – and invent your own. Most importantly, talk with the individuals and organizations whose capacity is being built, to find the most useful approaches.

Some of the tools suggested can be useful for every part of the organization; others will be appropriate for specific situations. Some could be used in building the capacity of financial staff, others for programme staff, still others for the leadership team.

Building relationships and communication

Good relationships and communication are the heart of any capacity-building initiatives. This is an ongoing process, and all the other tools depend on it.

A good relationship is especially important between finance and programme staff. Good or bad relationships can directly affect the quality of the programme.

In smaller organizations, this relationship generally works well. There are only a few people, and they see each other regularly, and so it is possible to communicate easily. As organizations grow, and especially as they start to form departments, communication may become more difficult. To maintain good communication, it is important for senior management to show that finance has a high priority and that they are personally disciplined in their financial work.

Giving encouragement

Remember to be positive about what is good. Sometimes it seems hard to find positive things to say, but people are much more likely to respond to being praised than being criticized.

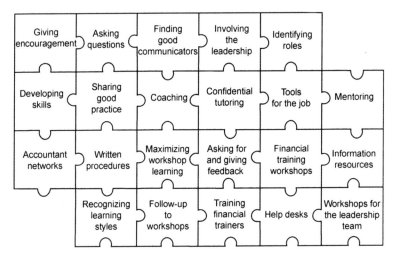

Figure 5 Tools for building financial management capacity

Find their strengths and tell people how much you appreciate the good practice that they are demonstrating. However, if working cross-culturally, check how appropriate public praise is – sometimes people will say 'so you mean I wasn't doing the work well before'. Gentle encouragement and affirmation are usually likely to be acceptable. Having done this, identifying and discussing the areas that need further work is more likely to be accepted and acted upon.

Asking questions

A powerful way of helping people to build their own capacity is to ask questions. Not only will this help the questioner, but the people answering them start to think about the way they do things, and about possible changes. The best questions lead people to build their own financial management capacity, without needing any external support.

Finding good communicators among finance staff

If you have good communicators among your finance staff, find opportunities to involve them in communicating financial information and funding issues with donors. These may be the people who can train and support others. It is worth investing in their development, possibly as financial trainers.

An example: The induction course for new staff included a session on travel expenses. One member of the finance team was always keen to take part. The training officer saw her potential and suggested that her skills could be used more widely. The finance person developed one-to-one financial training with the partner groups, which led to major improvements in their accounting.

Building the leadership's capacity

Involving the leadership

Financial management capacity building may fail if the leadership is not involved. One solution may be to work with the leadership team first. They can often become a catalyst for change in the organization. Such 'champions' might be, for example, the leader, a senior manager, or a member of the management committee.

An example: The finance officer tried to improve financial management capacity by introducing new systems. The director did not see the point of this, and no progress was made. A new member of the management committee was appointed who had a background in accounting. The finance officer convinced him that change was needed in the systems. The new committee member acted as a 'champion' by talking with the leader and senior staff, and the new systems were successfully introduced.

Confidential tutoring

Confidential tutoring can help if the leader, or manager, does not know how to manage financially. Rather than admit to a lack of knowledge, this person may delegate everything, saying that the finance team can be trusted to do it all. He or she is unlikely to attend a training course, because it would mean 'losing face'. This lack of involvement is likely to result in poor systems and major decisions being ill-informed. Eventually donors may stop funding because of the lack of good financial skills. If the issue is recognized, a possible solution is to arrange some confidential tutoring for the person concerned. The basics can be covered in a few sessions, and sometimes the tutor can then act as a mentor to the leader on financial issues.

Building staff capacity

Mentoring

What is mentoring?

The support of one individual by another on a regular basis. The aim is to empower the person being mentored to develop skills and build his or her confidence in dealing with unusual situations.

Someone with financial experience 'mentors' a member of staff. The mentor could be someone from the same or another organization doing similar work. Mentors and 'mentees' often meet monthly, sometimes more regularly in the early stages. This is a good way of building the confidence of individuals within the organization.

An example: Community-based organizations (CBOs) needed help in preparing their budget. The funding organization's programme officer was able to prepare her own budget, but needed to develop confidence in teaching the CBOs how to do it. After she had worked with a mentor, she was able to support the CBOs in a practical way. An experienced mentor met her to give her support before and after each CBO visit.

Coaching

What is coaching?

The use of one-to-one discussions to help a colleague find their own solutions using questioning, listening and feedback.

Source: Richards, 2005

Coaching is a way of talking with people about how they can find solutions to work problems. It involves two people: the 'coach' and the 'coachee'. They meet on a regular, although sometimes infrequent, basis. The coach has usually been trained to do this; it often needs no more than a day to learn the basics. Donors or commercial training organizations sometimes organize such training for coaches.

The coach does not need to know anything about finance in order to coach finance staff. Coaching is not about giving advice or being an 'expert'. It involves the coachees discovering the solutions themselves, and the coach being a facilitator to allow this to happen. Coaching builds financial management capacity by improving an individual's performance, confidence, and motivation. It increases staff retention, because people feel more valued. It can be used in many situations, with both finance and non-finance staff.

Sharing good practice

Members of staff have often worked elsewhere and seen good financial and management systems in place. Using good practice, they can help to professionalize their current organization and other groups with which they work.

Good practice often exists in neighbouring NGOs/CBOs. If this can be identified, it can be shared. It can be helpful to do this for an individual, but also with a staff team (in larger organizations), and between members of management committees. Many organizations have good practice that they can share, and if you are able to provide something for each other it can strengthen both organizations at little cost.

It might be helpful to organize learning visits between the finance people from two organizations or, if the organization is large enough, between two departments within the same organization. Donors can sometimes help to identify suitable organizations, and possibly fund any costs for visits between them.

An example: An organization saw finance as a 'policing' role: making sure that other staff always used the right budget and that expenditure was correctly authorized. The accounts were always excellent. Another organization saw the accounting role as 'supporting': making sure that programme staff achieved the results they wanted by finding ways of doing things that meant procedures had to become more flexible. Both ways had advantages, and by bringing these organizations together to exchange ideas, valuable learning took place.

Building the capacity of the finance team

Developing the skills of finance staff

Finance staff skills can be developed by others within their organization, or by an outside facilitator. First assess the gap between what is needed and what they are able to do, and decide whether on-the-job training would help.

Identifying roles for finance staff

Finance staff may be unsure what is expected of them: whether they are employed simply to keep records, or for something more.

Smaller organizations cannot usually afford highly trained finance staff, but the role still needs to be clarified so that staff can develop their skills and provide the best service to their organization. In larger organizations, qualified accounting staff often say that managers do not make the best use of their skills. Qualified accountants, for example, are trained to take part in long-term decision-making, as well as undertaking their financial role. Staff may leave if their roles are not made clear and are not fulfilling their personal needs and potential.

Accountant networks

In some countries, accountant networks for non-profit organizations are well established. If not, they can sometimes be introduced, either nationally or locally, by bringing together finance staff from different organizations. It works best if there is a specific reason for the meeting, for example a change in national regulations. This will encourage people to attend. The long-term benefit is often that participants will keep in touch and call on each other to discuss professional issues.

Tools for the job

Your finance staff need appropriate tools for their job. Tools vary according to circumstances: from small organizations needing a few handwritten records, to large organizations building a customized, computerized accounting system. As an organization grows, its needs to change and it should review and upgrade its tools.

An example: A small organization had relied on a few hand-written records, but now it was receiving external funding. The records were not detailed enough to provide donor reports. This was the time to start using a computer spreadsheet program with simple formats to keep the accounts and produce reports, both to the donor and to the organization's management committee and managers. Someone from a local organization offered to train staff in using computer spreadsheets.

Story: Tools for the job

A co-ordinator was concerned that his NGO could not access the financial information needed to run the organization and monitor its activities. He became critical of the book-keeper and said that she should be dismissed. His constant criticisms and misunderstandings annoyed the book-keeper, because she felt that she was doing her best to provide what she could with very limited resources.

To improve her own performance, the book-keeper then asked for support from the main donor's finance officer. She was introduced to simple tools for keeping accounts and preparing and monitoring the budget. The book-keeper worked with these tools, and the donor made follow-up visits, over a year or so. This helped to boost the book-keeper's confidence and helped her to identify her own position within the wider accounting role of the organization. She felt encouraged to keep up-to-date information, provide the required information to other staff in the organization, and give financial advice to the communities with which they worked.

The book-keeper is now a key person in the organization. She even feels able to challenge the new co-ordinator. She has put the organization in a strong financial position to approach other donors for funding. The new director and staff are delighted that the book-keeping role has been clarified, and that the tools are now available to provide the financial information required.

Source: Agir Autrement pour le Développement en Afrique, Senegal

---

Building resource capacity

Written financial procedures

Small organizations often operate without writing down how to do things, because everyone knows what to do. As organizations grow, they employ more people, and one person cannot remember everything. At this point, systems are usually written down. This helps to build financial management capacity. The writer has to think through and develop the systems; the information is then available for everyone to refer to; and new staff and volunteers have access to the information.

However, there may be limits to this. For example, an organization may distribute its written procedures but find that no one reads them. They may contain technical jargon, be badly written, or just be too long. Or it may simply be that the people for whom they were intended do not learn through reading (especially if the documents are written in their second language).

Some organizations find it useful to provide instructions about financial procedures on a 'need-to-know' basis. When the budgeting process starts, for example, this section of the procedures is circulated. The aim is to receive the right information, at the right level, at the right time. Other organizations communicate their basic procedures in a visual and/or verbal presentation at a group meeting. It is important to make sure that anyone who does not read or write is not left out. These meetings allow the issues to be discussed and questions to be raised by the people who will use them.

Information resources

Much general financial information is available in written and electronic formats. There are lists of 'Written resources' and 'Web resources' at the end of this book. Staff should be encouraged to use these and other resources for self-development. Make sure that the resources are easily available to, and used by, all staff and not just kept in the leader's office.

Smaller organizations cannot always afford to buy printed or electronic resources. Donors will often offer specific funding for this purpose, if an item is entered in the budget. Talk to your donor about this.

Help desks

Large organizations sometimes offer a telephone or email 'help desk' for financial queries within their organization. Donors sometimes provide smaller organizations with a similar service; for example, there may be a formal or informal arrangement with their donor's accountant. Sometimes donors provide a social media presence, which invites and answers queries. This can allow immediate communication with the staff of donors and other organizations.

Asking for and giving feedback

Being open to feedback from others is a useful way of building financial management capacity. The feedback may come from members of your own or a partner organization, community groups, staff, volunteers, and donors. It may also come from formal reviews, for example an evaluation or audit. It may be as an indication of how well you have built financial management capacity. For example, you might ask users questions such as: 'How satisfied are you with the financial reports you receive?' 'How could you improve them?' Or you might wish to record information that tells you what proportion of financial reports are produced and distributed in a specific time period; for example, one week after the end of the month. Feedback needs to be taken seriously: decide how valid the suggestions are and then, if appropriate, respond to them.

Feedback given to others can be a powerful way of building their capacity too. However, remember to give any criticism carefully and in a way that provides a better way of doing things. Provide positive feedback before and after the negative. Always try and allow people to avoid 'losing face' and embarrassment.

An example: An organization asked for feedback about the financial services provided over two weeks each year. There was a written questionnaire with three simple questions, which some people completed. Most feedback was gathered verbally when people came to the office. At the end of the two weeks, the information was gathered together and presented to a meeting of staff. Suggestions for improvements were then followed up, resulting in positive changes in the way the finance team worked.

CHAPTER 12

Training for financial management capacity building

Training is often used as a method of capacity building. This chapter considers how to use financial training; the use of follow-ups to workshops; how we might maximize the learning; and how we might train finance staff to become trainers themselves.

Keywords: training to build non-profit financial management capacity; non-profit financial management training workshops; facilitating financial training workshops; follow-up to training; training financial trainers

Capacity building with financial training workshops

Training workshops provide an input for a larger group of people than would be possible with on-the-job training. Participants meet people who do similar work in other organizations.

Workshops can be organized and funded by larger donors for a number of their partners. They can also be run by organizations internally and for their community groups, or by 'umbrella' groups for other non-profit organizations. Box 22 gives some guidance on the use of workshops.

Participatory training approaches (which actively involve participants in the training, rather than just talking at them) are essential for training in financial subjects. Courses should provide 'hands-on' experience of the task to be learned. The trainer should provide an outline programme before the course, describing the course aims and objectives, and clear, well-written support materials for people to take away after the course. If you are inviting outside speakers to take part in the training, check beforehand that they too will present their material in a participatory way.

For non-literate groups, use diagrams, verbal and visual activities, and objects to give the quantity and value that you want to show participants. If it is essential to have some things written down, it may be possible for participants to invite a literate relative or friend to accompany them. It is helpful to use visual activities for all course participants.

People who attend financial training may feel threatened by the process. It may remind them of school mathematics lessons. They may fear looking foolish. Trainers have to work hard to reassure course participants, and they should be positive, not critical, in their approach. Tell participants that you will always start off with the basics and gradually build on this using a step-by-step approach – and then do so.

Box 22 Thinking of using a workshop to build financial management capacity?

GREEN – go ahead

- if you have fully assessed the training needs;
- if the training is a part of other capacity building initiatives;
- if the members of the group have similar backgrounds and experience;
- to increase the profile of finance within the organization(s);
- to encourage senior managers and management committee members to develop financial management capacity building skills;
- to encourage non-finance people to use financial management skills;
- to develop the skills of finance staff.

AMBER – be careful

- if you haven't first considered other approaches to financial management capacity building;
- if the workshop is not really relevant to the needs of the participants;
- if the facilitator cannot use participatory training methods.

RED – don't proceed

- if you think a workshop will solve all your problems;
- if you expect that it will simply make people do what you want them to;
- if other approaches to financial management capacity building will work better.

Use simple formats for examples, remembering that people will often be seeing them for the first time. Once they are familiar with these formats, you can go on to slightly more complex examples. If possible, don't use technical language; but if you do use any, explain it first. Box 23 offers some guidelines to facilitators of financial training workshops.

Box 23 Facilitating financial training workshops

Do

- Prepare thoroughly.
- Be realistic about what is possible in the time available.
- State the purpose of each session.
- Deliver financial training with energy and enthusiasm.
- Start off each topic with the basics.
- Follow a logical pattern.
- Give out written materials as appropriate to support the sessions.
- Get the group doing things – don't talk too long.
- Ask, and invite, questions.
- Encourage participants – be positive.
- Use a variety of methods – and have fun!

Don't

- Try to guess what the group already knows. If unsure, ask them.
- Use technical terms unless you first explain them.
- Rush the presentation or talk too fast.
- Try to cover everything.
- Make a participant feel that he or she has failed.

Make sure that financial workshops are open to all parts of the communities or organizations with which you work. A wide variety of people can do financial tasks, but most need support and training to help them to achieve their full potential and benefit their community or organization.

The outcome of workshops should be that participants feel more confident about the financial work of the organization, and about their role within it. Also, after the workshop a much better relationship often develops between participants and the financial people who have facilitated such learning.

Follow-up to workshops

The best workshops include some follow-up by the facilitator. This is especially important for participants from smaller organizations. If, for example, the workshop is about basic accounting records, a visit to see how the participants are getting on and to give individual advice would be particularly helpful, about a month or so after the workshop. This follow-up may lead to further visits or to mentoring participants.

Follow-up of learning can be more effective than a one-off workshop, because it makes sure that the learning is fully understood. It can be expensive, but some larger organizations or donors are willing to fund follow-up activities.

Story: Training and follow-up

Training for organizations needs more than a one-off course. The Copperbelt Health Education Project (CHEP) provides workshops for the communities it works with in basic financial skills, resource mobilization, and management of income-generating activities. The financial workshops cover topics such as completing accounting documents and cash/bank books, preparing bank reconciliations, and compiling financial reports to donors.

At the end of each workshop, the participants complete an action plan of tasks to carry out when they return to their organization. During the meeting to review the action plan after the workshop, CHEP's staff check progress on agreed tasks – for example: 'Establishing an equipment register in the format taught during the training'. CHEP staff follow up this training with 'mentoring' and 'monitoring' visits to each of the participants.

The mentoring visit usually takes place two weeks after the course or workshop. It aims to discover whether the training has been effective in the participant's work situation. A typical visit would check that documentation exists for every stage of ordering goods. The community-based organizations (CBOs) are helped to develop project proposals. CBOs are also taught how to manage small business initiatives to contribute to their organization's sustainability.

After the first mentoring visit, there are follow-up 'monitoring' visits to make sure that things are running smoothly. Further visits and telephone and email contact are then arranged for as long as needed.

Source: Copperbelt Health Education Project, Zambia

Maximizing workshop learning

All workshops should be used as an opportunity to pass on learning to others. Not only is this helpful for those who did not attend, but it reinforces the learning for those who did.

For participants on a course, a session towards the end of preparing an 'action plan' helps to focus on what they can take away to use in their daily work. This can be for their personal use, or shared with the facilitator. It can become a checklist for actions, and the facilitator might use this as the basis to follow up the training. This might be by a visit, a telephone call or email, or all of these. Sometimes a email/postal reminder is sent to all participants a few weeks after the course so they can review their actions for themselves.

A useful approach is to develop the practice of requiring each participant to report what they have learned back to their team. This can be a brief report of the main highlights, supported, if possible, by materials copied for others to see. Workshop organizers can encourage this practice by including the question 'How will you pass this learning on to others?' on evaluation forms.

Some organizations send two people to financial training sessions, for example the leader and the finance person. Both benefit, and it also helps to provide continuity if one of them leaves the organization later.

Different learning styles

It is sometimes assumed that everyone learns in the same way. This is not true. If the information that you want to share is important, plan to present it in different ways that will reach everybody, whatever their preferred learning style. Don't assume that everyone learns in the same way that you do! In some cultures, it is more natural to learn face-to-face than through the written word. The best way is to ask those involved, 'How do you prefer to learn?'

Some of the different ways of acquiring new skills are listed below:

- on-the-job training;
- books and other written information;
- face-to-face instruction and discussions;
- by teaching someone else;
- participation in external courses, whether at a college, or by means of distance-learning or e-learning through the internet;
- short training sessions as part of regular work meetings;
- networking with other people doing similar work;
- interactive computer packages.

Financial workshops for senior managers and management committee members

Workshops for the leadership team are less usual, but they can be an effective way of making change happen. If other methods of financial management capacity building have not worked, it is worth asking whether training at this level would help.

The leadership and management committee members are busy people, so it is important to limit the time involved to one or two days – whatever is possible – which means prioritizing the material. For management committee members, the training may need to be fitted into their regular meetings. It is especially important to get the best facilitator available.

Training financial trainers

Building financial management capacity relies on the skills of individuals. People with financial skills do not always have the skills to train others. It is important to invest in training staff as financial trainers, if this is part of their job, and especially if they have the potential to be good trainers. General courses in the training of trainers are widely available. Some specialist courses are available for finance trainers; they help to develop skills and focus on ways of communicating financial management in a participatory way.

Minimum financial requirements for growing organizations

http://dx.doi.org/10.3362/9781780448244.005

Stage of development	Early life	Growing up	Adulthood	Maturity
Possible situation	Group of volunteers; no commitments beyond immediate work; local fundraising; no donor funding; whole group acts as the management committee	A few paid staff, rented premises; few financial commitments; one donor; management committee formed	More paid staff, own premises, equipment, and vehicles; financial commitments to communities and/or partners; several donors	Many paid staff, premises, vehicles, and equipment; financial commitments to partners; many donors
Planning and budgeting	Decide objectives A basic budget	Detailed budget to suit donor's format Cash-flow forecast Budget and actual reports produced for management committee	Detailed planning Budgets for each donor and one for the whole organization Budget and actual reports for managers Funding/financing plan	Long-term planning An organizational budget, showing donor funding Detailed reports available for management
Accounts record keeping	Cash transactions Bank account Own records agreed with bank statement	Paper-based or computer spreadsheet record keeping	Computerized accounting package Advances/loans and other registers	Custom-made accounting system Non-finance staff have access to read-only computerized accounting records
Financial reporting	Summary of money received and spent presented to meetings	Donor reports Annual accounting statements Providing community or partner reports	Accounts showing restricted and unrestricted funds	Detailed annual report and accounting statements

Stage of development	Early life	Growing up	Adulthood	Maturity
Financial controls	Two signatories on cheques	Basic controls	Comprehensive financial controls Written financial procedures	Detailed financial controls throughout organization
External audit	Independent review	Financial audit	Management audit	Audit examines programme activities
Staffing	Group member deals with the finances	Administrator appointed Professional accountant to prepare end-of-year accounts	Book-keeper appointed	Professional accounting staff
Things to think about	How to raise more funds	The need for reserves What could go wrong	Financial training for non-finance staff A reserves policy New ways of paying for core costs	Possibility of refusing donor funding Possible risks Encouraging partner organizations to develop their financial systems

Each organization is different and each stage builds on and includes what has happened before. This table offers a summary of the additional systems that can be introduced at each stage of growth.

Review of financial systems

Notes on using the review

This review helps you to assess your organization's financial systems and identify its strengths and weaknesses. A minimum standard is given for each question. The review is a way of identifying improvements that can be made to strengthen your financial and management capacity, rather than a way of judging the organization.

- If you score many 1s and 2s, you are likely to need some urgent action, and possibly to call on outside help.
- If you score mostly 4s and 5s, you have good financial systems, but there may still be some matters needing attention.

The best person to complete the review is someone who knows the organization well. He or she can offer comments on most questions, or at least know where to find the information. Some questions will need to be answered by a senior person who understands the management committee. It is important that answers are as honest as possible, describing what actually happens, rather than what you think should happen.

It works best if someone inside the organization conducts the review, rather than someone from outside. However, an external facilitator who is helping to build capacity can introduce it, as long as there is enough trust between them and the organization.

Not every question is appropriate for every organization, and you can add your own questions at the end. Small voluntary community-based organizations, for example, may not need all the systems covered in the review.

As you go along, write down comments in the column headed 'Any action needed'. When you have finished the review, write down the action points as a checklist, with a date by which you want to achieve them. Send a copy to all concerned.

A downloadable copy of this review is available at www.johncammack.net (click on 'Resources').

Review of financial systems

For each question, circle the number that most closely matches the present situation.

1 = Never, or don't know 2 = Rarely 3 = Occasionally 4 = Sometimes 5 = Always

Compare the response with the 'minimum standard' and write down 'any action needed'.

Technical terms are **highlighted** and explained in the Glossary at the start of the book.

Question	Rating	Minimum standard	Any action needed
A. PLANNING AND BUDGETING			
1. Is an annual budget prepared and approved by the management committee?	1 2 3 4 5	The budget is prepared after talking with staff/other stakeholders. The management committee approves it, and checks that confirmed income covers expenditure.	
2. Is the budget based on current objectives?	1 2 3 4 5	The budget is based on current objectives.	
3. Do all relevant staff/volunteers discuss the budget details?	1 2 3 4 5	Relevant staff/volunteers are consulted about and/or contribute to budget discussions. Smaller organizations may include all their staff/volunteers.	
4. Are budgets finalized before the start of the financial year/project period?	1 2 3 4 5	The process is started early enough for it to be ready before the year/project starts.	
5. Are notes added to the budget, justifying items and showing calculations?	1 2 3 4 5	The person responsible for the budget adds notes.	
6. Does the budget avoid having more expenditure than income, unless this is planned?	1 2 3 4 5	If the budget shows that a deficit is likely, budgeted expenditure is reduced until more income is raised.	
7. Is a **cash-flow forecast** prepared, especially when there is not enough money?	1 2 3 4 5	A forecast is prepared regularly, and every time funds may run out. Good practice is to prepare a forecast which is updated each month.	

Question	Rating	Minimum standard	Any action needed
8. Do the management committee and leader regularly review a summary of the **budget and actual statement?**	1 2 3 4 5	Management committee regularly review the budget and actual statement. They ask questions about large differences between budget and actual figures.	
9. Do managers regularly review their expenditure/income against budget?	1 2 3 4 5	Managers review the budget and actual statement monthly/quarterly to make sure they are spending within budget.	
10. Are explanations for large differences between budget and actual noted on the budget and actual statement?	1 2 3 4 5	The person managing the budget writes notes on the budget and actual statement to explain large differences.	
11. Are budget and actual reports produced quickly after the period-end?	1 2 3 4 5	Budget and actual statements are produced within two weeks of the period-end. The management committee/leader/manager can then act quickly.	
12. Are meetings held between finance people and managers to discuss the contents of the budget and actual report?	1 2 3 4 5	Meetings, either one-to-one or in a group, are held immediately after the information is produced.	
B. ACCOUNTS RECORD KEEPING			
1. Is the record of transactions (the **cash/ bank book**) updated regularly?	1 2 3 4 5	The cash/bank book is updated daily, or whenever money is paid in or out. An up-to-date balance can always be calculated.	
2. Is every cash/bank book entry supported by, for example, an invoice or receipt?	1 2 3 4 5	Documents are kept and filed. If there is no external document, a **payment voucher** is written, showing the details, which a senior person approves.	

Question	Rating	Minimum standard	Any action needed
3. Are financial documents filed in order?	1 2 3 4 5	Separate files are kept for money received and money paid. Documents are cross-referenced to the cash/bank book.	
4. Is money received banked as soon as possible?	1 2 3 4 5	Money is banked as often as possible, depending on how much and how close the bank is.	
5. Is a separate register kept, listing money given as a **cash advance** or as a loan to staff?	1 2 3 4 5	A **cash advances/loans register** lists all advances/loans and records when they are issued, accounted for, and repaid. It can easily show amounts outstanding, to be followed up. Loan repayments are deducted from salaries.	
6. Do the accounting records show donor funds given for a particular purpose?	1 2 3 4 5	Accounting records clearly show if funds are **restricted**. If funding is complicated and/or there are several donors, an extra system makes sure that restricted funds are monitored accurately.	
7. Is there a record to make sure that money due is all received and is on time?	1 2 3 4 5	Extra accounting records show money due and when it is paid, even if only in a notebook.	
8. Is a list of budget codes used to prepare the budget, and charge expenditure correctly?	1 2 3 4 5	The list of codes may be given by a computerized accounting package or by a donor. It may need to be customized.	
9. Is cash kept securely?	1 2 3 4 5	There is a safe or locked cupboard. No more cash is kept than is needed.	
10. Is the cash balance monitored?	1 2 3 4 5	Someone takes action when the cash balance becomes too low.	

Question	Rating	Minimum standard	Any action needed
11. Is a pre-numbered receipt issued for cash received?	1 2 3 4 5	Receipts are pre-numbered and show the organization's name. The original is given to the person paying in the cash, and a copy is kept.	
12. Does someone other than the cashier authorize payments?	1 2 3 4 5	The cashier only pays with authorized documents.	
13. Does a senior person count the cash regularly?	1 2 3 4 5	A senior person agrees the cash balance with the cash/bank book at least weekly (on a different day each week).	
14. Are bank accounts registered in the organization's name?	1 2 3 4 5	All accounts are in the name of the organization/project.	
15. Is there a separate cash/bank book for each bank account?	1 2 3 4 5	There is a cash/bank book for each bank account.	
16. Has each bank account at least two signatories?	1 2 3 4 5	Each account has at least two people to sign cheques. If they are sometimes unavailable, more people will be needed.	
17. Do two people sign cheques and payment instructions?	1 2 3 4 5	Two people sign each cheque/payment instruction. This prevents errors and theft.	
18. Are cheques signed after the details are entered?	1 2 3 4 5	'Blank' cheques should never be signed.	
19. Is a **bank reconciliation** prepared every time a statement is received or the pass book updated?	1 2 3 4 5	A bank reconciliation is completed regularly, to agree the bank statement with the cash/bank book.	
20. Does the leader/manager approve the bank reconciliation?	1 2 3 4 5	The leader or a manager approves the bank reconciliation.	

Question	Rating	Minimum standard	Any action needed
21. Are cheques used as often as possible?	1 2 3 4 5	Cheques, not cash, are used whenever possible.	
22. Are cheque books kept securely?	1 2 3 4 5	Cheque books are kept in a safe or locked cupboard.	
23. Do cancelled cheques have 'cancelled' written on them, and are they kept for audit?	1 2 3 4 5	Cheques are cancelled when necessary, kept, and filed.	
24. Is there a list of all paid staff?	1 2 3 4 5	A staff list is kept up to date.	
25. Are staff taken off the payroll as soon as they leave?	1 2 3 4 5	There is a procedure for making sure no one can be paid after they have left. Someone other than the person responsible for paying the salaries checks this.	
26. Do staff sign for salaries received in cash?	1 2 3 4 5	Staff always sign a receipt when they receive a salary in cash.	
27. Are legal deductions calculated and paid to the appropriate authorities promptly?	1 2 3 4 5	Deductions required by law are made and paid when salaries are paid.	
28. Are extra accounting records kept, for example ledger, journal, sales and purchase records, if needed?	1 2 3 4 5	Larger organizations need extra records, appropriate for their size/activities.	
C. FINANCIAL REPORTING			
1. Are annual accounting statements prepared, and do they show **restricted** and **unrestricted** funds?	1 2 3 4 5	Annual summaries of income and expenditure are produced. Larger organizations also have more detailed statements. Both statements show which funds are restricted for a particular use.	

Question	Rating	Minimum standard	Any action needed
2. Do the management committee review and approve the annual accounting statements?	1 2 3 4 5	The management committee review and approve annual statements.	
3. Can the accounting system produce donor reports in the required format?	1 2 3 4 5	Accounting systems produce donor reports in the required format.	
4. Are donor reports always prepared on time?	1 2 3 4 5	Donor reports are prepared and sent on time.	
5. Do donors receive a copy of the annual accounting statements?	1 2 3 4 5	There is a list of donors, and annual accounting statements are sent to donors and other stakeholders.	
6. Are financial information and reports used to plan for the future?	1 2 3 4 5	Financial reports are used to plan future programmes.	
D. FINANCIAL CONTROLS			
1. Are financial tasks separated?	1 2 3 4 5	No one person does the whole of any one financial transaction. This is to prevent errors and theft.	
2. Is expenditure authorized by a senior staff member (or the leader)?	1 2 3 4 5	Expenditure is approved before it is paid. Someone asks 'Where is it in the budget?'	
3. Are there limits on how much expenditure staff can authorize?	1 2 3 4 5	There are limits, and all staff, especially finance staff, know them.	
4. Do different people authorize payments and sign cheques for those payments?	1 2 3 4 5	No one person can authorize a payment and sign a cheque for the same transaction.	
5. Is there a list of authorized signatories, including their level of authorization?	1 2 3 4 5	A signatories list is available.	

Question	Rating	Minimum standard	Any action needed
6. Are payments made only with an original invoice?	1 2 3 4 5	There is a system to avoid duplicate payments.	
7. Is the invoice checked against the original order, to help prevent double payment?	1 2 3 4 5	Purchase orders are attached to invoices, or a similar system is in place.	
8. Are several quotes asked for when making large purchases of goods or services?	1 2 3 4 5	Three quotes are required for goods or services (possibly only for items above a certain amount).	
9. Does someone check that goods and services are received and in good condition before they are paid for?	1 2 3 4 5	The invoice is signed to show that the goods/ services have been received and are of acceptable quality.	
10. Is a record of what is owned (**fixed assets**) kept up to date and reviewed regularly?	1 2 3 4 5	A **fixed-asset register** is kept for details of items owned. This includes the date of purchase, the value, and where they were bought and are kept. This is agreed annually with the actual items.	
11. Is there enough insurance to cover the current value of what is owned, and for other risks?	1 2 3 4 5	Items owned are fully insured. Other risks (for example public liability, fire and theft, and cash in transit) should also be covered, if this is possible in the country where you work.	
12. Can items be replaced easily when they wear out?	1 2 3 4 5	There is/will be funding to replace essential items.	
13. Is everything owned kept securely?	1 2 3 4 5	Valuable items are locked or kept in locked rooms.	
14. Is financial stationery numbered, named, and held securely?	1 2 3 4 5	All financial stationery is kept in a safe or locked cupboard.	

Question	Rating	Minimum standard	Any action needed
15. Are the entrances to the premises and stores secured?	1 2 3 4 5	Premises are locked and (if necessary) guarded.	
16. Is there a log book to record mileage for each vehicle?	1 2 3 4 5	Drivers complete the vehicle log book each time a journey is made.	
17. Do staff pay for personal use of telephones and photocopiers?	1 2 3 4 5	Staff know the organizational policy and how to pay for use.	
18. Are a stock register and records kept?	1 2 3 4 5	There is a basic system of stock control, for example for medical supplies.	
19. Is stock counted regularly, and agreed with the stock register?	1 2 3 4 5	An independent person carries out stock counts at least every three months.	
E. EXTERNAL AUDIT ASSESSMENT			
1. Do the management committee select the auditors yearly?	1 2 3 4 5	Appointing the auditors is on the management committee's agenda each year.	
2. Does a financial audit/independent review take place each year?	1 2 3 4 5	An independent person/auditing firm conducts a yearly financial audit.	
3. Is the audit firm (or are individual auditors within the same firm) changed every four or five years?	1 2 3 4 5	The audit firm, or the individual responsible within a firm, is replaced every four to five years.	
4. Does the auditor provide a letter giving recommendations?	1 2 3 4 5	The auditor makes recommendations (the 'management letter') to the management committee at the end of the audit.	
5. Does the management committee see the auditor's recommendations and take the necessary action?	1 2 3 4 5	Recommendations are implemented and followed up.	

Question	Rating	Minimum standard	Any action needed
6. Does the auditor provide a **management (or systems) audit?**	1 2 3 4 5	The auditor looks at financial and management systems and the use of management information.	
F. MANAGEMENT COMMITTEE			
1. Does one member of the management committee take the lead on financial issues?	1 2 3 4 5	One member of the management committee is responsible for financial issues.	
2. Can members of the management committee understand basic financial information, or are they being trained to do so?	1 2 3 4 5	At least one other person, besides the lead financial person, is competent to ask questions about financial information at meetings.	
G. FINANCE STAFF			
1. Are finance staff competent?	1 2 3 4 5	Finance staff have suitable training and/or experience.	
2. Are job descriptions available for all finance staff?	1 2 3 4 5	All staff have job descriptions.	
3. Are qualifications and references checked before new staff are appointed?	1 2 3 4 5	References and qualifications are always checked.	
4. Do interviewees take a practical test of their financial skills?	1 2 3 4 5	Tests are used to assess skills when candidates are interviewed for finance posts.	
5. Are staff encouraged to take further training?	1 2 3 4 5	Someone is responsible for encouraging staff development.	
6. Is the number and experience level of staff enough for the organization's activities?	1 2 3 4 5	There are enough appropriately trained staff, especially when large amounts of additional funding is received.	

Question	Rating	Minimum standard	Any action needed
7. Are some staff able to communicate effectively to a non-finance audience?	1 2 3 4 5	At least one person can explain financial information and its impact on the organization.	
8. Do interviews include a test on how well finance staff can communicate in everyday language with non-finance people?	1 2 3 4 5	Interviews for key finance staff include an opportunity to test how well they communicate with non-finance people.	
9. Is there continuity of staff?	1 2 3 4 5	There is enough continuity. If high turnover is due to low salaries, the leadership team should consider other ways of valuing/keeping staff.	
H. FINANCIAL INFORMATION			
1. Is the information given to the management committee, leader, and managers up to date?	1 2 3 4 5	Information is available within two weeks of the period-end.	
2. Is information presented in a user-friendly format?	1 2 3 4 5	The management committee can understand a summary of the budget and actual statement; managers have a more detailed version.	
3. Are financial policies and procedures put in writing?	1 2 3 4 5	Except for very small organizations, written procedures are available.	
I. CULTURE			
1. Does the management committee prioritize financial matters at their meetings?	1 2 3 4 5	The management committee/senior staff receive regular financial reports at their meetings.	
2. Does the leader prioritize finance and encourage everyone else to do the same?	1 2 3 4 5	Staff and volunteers know that high standards of financial management are expected.	

Question	Rating	Minimum standard	Any action needed
3. Does the leader submit his/her financial forms quickly?	1 2 3 4 5	The leader sets a good example.	
4. Are programme staff and other staff aware of financial issues?	1 2 3 4 5	Staff are confident to do the financial tasks in their job description.	
5. Is there a numerical test at interviews for non-financial staff who have financial responsibilities in their job description?	1 2 3 4 5	Numerical tests are used to assess existing skills and/or show what training is needed.	
J. EXTERNAL RELATIONSHIPS			
1. Do the management committee and the leader consider external risks?	1 2 3 4 5	The yearly planning process includes time to consider what could go wrong.	
2. Is there a strong, transparent relationship with communities, partners, donors, and other stakeholders?	1 2 3 4 5	The organization, its communities, partners and donors can all obtain answers to their financial/general questions, in an open and friendly way.	
3. Do stakeholders trust the financial management?	1 2 3 4 5	Stakeholders trust the organization's financial systems and staff.	
4. Do stakeholders (including communities and/or partners) receive regular financial reports in a suitable format?	1 2 3 4 5	All stakeholders, including communities and partners, receive appropriate information about financial aspects of the work.	
5. Do finance staff meet with communities/ partners to discuss financial matters?	1 2 3 4 5	Depending on the size and style of the organization, finance staff and communities/ partners can talk with each other about financial matters.	

Question	Rating	Minimum standard	Any action needed
K. SUSTAINABILITY			
1. Does longer-term planning happen?	1 2 3 4 5	Longer-term objectives and/or a **strategic plan** has been/is being adopted by the management committee and other stakeholders, and implemented.	
2. Is there a **financing plan/fundraising** plan?	1 2 3 4 5	A financing plan/fundraising plan has been/is being adopted by the management committee, and implemented.	
3. Is there a policy for funding **core costs**?	1 2 3 4 5	The management committee have considered this, although it may be difficult to find an ideal solution.	
4. Has the organization considered whether it needs a **reserves** fund and policy?	1 2 3 4 5	Reserves funds have been discussed. If they are needed and possible, there are plans and a policy for establishing and maintaining them.	
5. If donor funding were to stop immediately, could the organization continue until new funds were raised?	1 2 3 4 5	Enough funds are available to pay essential costs until new sources of income can be identified and money received.	
6. Are donors' funds used only in accordance with their wishes?	1 2 3 4 5	A system for accounting for restricted funds is in place (see also question B6).	
7. Have sources of income other than donor funds been considered?	1 2 3 4 5	Options for financing other than donor funds have been considered.	

Question	Rating	Minimum standard	Any action needed
	1 2 3 4 5		
	1 2 3 4 5		
	1 2 3 4 5		
	1 2 3 4 5		
	1 2 3 4 5		
	1 2 3 4 5		
	1 2 3 4 5		
	1 2 3 4 5		

Action points

Date of review of action points ....

Signed .... Date ....

Signed .... Date ....

References

Bruty, B. (2005) 'Guidance notes: core funding strategies', London: British Overseas NGOs for Development (Bond), based on research by Mike Hudson (1999) in *Managing without Profit*, London: Penguin Books.

Camfed International (2004) *Camfed Annual Review 2003/04*, Cambridge: Camfed International.

Cammack, J. (2000), *Financial Management for Development*, Oxford: International NGO Training and Research Centre (Intrac).

Cammack, J. (2012) *Communicating Financial Management with Non-finance People: A Manual for International Development Workers*, Rugby, UK: Practical Action Publishing.

Cammack, J., Foster, T. and Hale, S. (2005) *Financial Management for Emergencies: A Survival Guide for Humanitarian Programme Managers* [online] <www.fme-online.org>.

Charity Commission (2008) *Accounting and Reporting by Charities: Statement of Recommended Practice*, London: Charity Commission.

Clark, C. (2001) *Managing Risk: Guidelines for Medium-sized Voluntary Organisations*, London: National Council for Voluntary Organisations.

Environmental Support Center and Innovation Network (2002) *Echoes from the Field: Proven Capacity-building Principles for Nonprofits*, Washington, DC: Environmental Support Center and Innovation Network <www.innonet.org/resources/node/172>.

Methodist Relief and Development Fund (2011) 'Strength to Strength newsletter: strategic planning', Issue 11 (January), London: MRDF.

Richards, S. (2005) 'ITC Coaching for Senior Managers', London: Independent Theatre Council <www.sianrichards.com>.

Tools for Self Reliance (2005) *Tools for Self-reliance Annual Report*, Southampton: Tools for Self Reliance.

Written resources

Accounting and financial management

Cammack, J. (2000) *Financial Management for Development: Accounting and Finance for the Non-specialist in Development Organisations*, Oxford: International NGO Training and Research Centre (Intrac).

Cammack, J. (2014) *Basic Accounting for Community Organizations and Small Groups: A Practical Guide*, Rugby, UK: Practical Action Publishing.

Collins, R. (1994) *Management Controls for Development Organisations, Part 1 and 2*, Crediton, UK: Stephen Sims and Partners.

Gupta, K.N. (2004) *Manual of Financial Management and Legal Regulations*, Delhi: Financial Management Services Foundation.

Sayer, K. (2007) *A Practical Guide to Financial Management*, London: Directory of Social Change.

Capacity building and financial communication

Cammack, J. (2012) *Communicating Financial Management with Non-finance People: A Manual for International Development Workers*, Rugby, UK: Practical Action Publishing.

Crooks, B. (2003) *Capacity Self-assessment*, Teddington: Tearfund.

Cutts, M. (2009) *Oxford Guide to Plain English*, Oxford: Oxford University Press.

Eade, D. (1997) *Capacity building: An Approach to People-centred Development*, Oxford: Oxfam GB.

James, R. and Hailey, J. (2007) *Capacity Building for NGOs: Making it Work*, Oxford: International NGO Training and Research Centre (Intrac).

Organizational sustainability

Botting Herbst, N. and Norton, M. (2012) *The Complete Fundraising Handbook*, London: Directory of Social Change.

Cammack, J. (2013) 'Considered choices for funding decisions: how to calculate the real cost of donor-funded projects; when to say "yes" and when to say "no"', *Development in Practice* 23 (4): 589–95 <http://dx.doi.org/10.1080/09614524.2013.790943>.

ChildHope (2010) *Strategic Planning for Non-government Organisations: A Training Workbook Guidelines and Toolkit*, London: ChildHope.

Fiennes, C., Langerman, C., Vlahovic, J. and ACEVO (2009) *Full Cost Recovery: A Guide and Toolkit on Cost Allocation version 2 (Understanding the Full-cost Business Planner)*, London: ACEVO and New Philanthropy Capital.

Holloway, R. (2001) *Towards Financial Self-Reliance: A Handbook on Resource Mobilization for Civil Society Organizations in the South*, London: Earthscan, Civicus and Aga Khan Foundation. Also *Trainer Manual* (see Web resources).

Norton, M. (2009) *The Worldwide Fundraiser's Handbook*, London: Directory of Social Change.

Training

Chambers, R. (2002) *Participatory Workshops*, London: Earthscan.

Guijt, I., Pretty, J.N., Scoones, I. and Thompson, J. (1995) *Participatory Learning and Action – a Trainer's Guide,* London: International Institute of Environment and Development.

Lead International (2004) *Training Across Cultures: A Handbook for Trainers and Facilitators Working Around the World*, London: Lead International.

Web resources

Financial management

www.bond.org.uk (click on 'resources'/search keywords 'how to')
    Bond 'How to …' guides on project budgeting and other topics
www.civicus.org (click on 'resources'/'toolkits')
    Civicus 'toolkits' include finance topics
www.fme-online.org
    Financial Management for Emergencies provides good practice
    and examples of formats for accounting in development organiza-
    tions as well as emergencies
www.johncammack.net (click on 'links' and 'resources')
    Links to sites about accounting and financial management, spread-
    sheet templates for budgeting, and article on gender budgeting
www.mango.org.uk
    Accounting and financial resources
www.ncvo-vol.org.uk (click on 'practical support'/'financial
    management' and 'funding')
    Resources about financial management and financing organizations
www.ngomanager.org (click on 'library'/'e-library')
    Resources on managing finance

Capacity building and financial communication

www.capacity.org
    Resources for capacity building
www.ngoconnect.net
    Resources for assessing organizational capacity
www.intrac.org
    Resources for organizational capacity building
www.johncammack.net (click on 'links' and 'resources')
    Extra resources for this book, useful research, and web links
www.plainenglish.co.uk (click on 'plain English tools free guides')
    Good practice in writing plain English

Organizational sustainability

www.aidsalliance.org (click on 'resources'/'key resources')
   Guides on 'CBO capacity analysis', 'NGO capacity analysis' and
   'How to develop a strategic plan: a guide for NGOs and CBOs'
www.akdn.org (click on 'publications', search for 'toolkits')
   Towards Financial Self-Reliance: A Handbook on Resource Mobilization
   for Civil Society Organizations in the South: Trainer Manual by Richard
   Holloway <www.akdn.org/publications/akf_toolkit_manual.pdf>
www.civicus.org (click on 'resources'/'toolkits')
   Civicus 'toolkits' include longer-term planning and financing
www.gdnet.org (click on 'learning and publications'/'GDNet Toolkits'/
   'proposal writing and fundraising')
   Tips and suggestions for applying for funds and proposal writing
www.mango.org.uk (click on 'guide' and 'financial sustainability')
   Information about becoming financially sustainable
www.mindtools.com (click on 'toolkits' and 'strategy tools')
   Resources about SWOT analysis and other planning tools
www.networklearning.org
   Information on building sustainability, funding and longer-term
   strategic planning
www.progressio.org.uk (click on 'publications')
   Capacity Building for Local NGOs: A Guidance Manual for Good Practice
   <www.progressio.org.uk/content/capacity-building-manual>

Training

www.aidsalliance.org (click on 'resources'/'key resources')
Guide on '100 ways to energize groups: games to use in workshops,
   meetings and the community'
www.ica-sae.org (click on 'Training the Trainer resource pack')
   Training the Trainer resource pack
www.trainingzone.co.uk
   Tips on a range of training topics
www.thiagi.com
   Free games for participatory training

Index

Lightning Source UK Ltd.
Milton Keynes UK
UKOW05f1504120814

236836UK00001B/7/P